A C   CB

Youth Mentoring

A Guide to
Youth Mentoring

Providing Effective Social Support

Pat Dolan and Bernadine Brady

Jessica Kingsley *Publishers*
London and Philadelphia

First published in 2012
by Jessica Kingsley Publishers
116 Pentonville Road
London N1 9JB, UK
and
400 Market Street, Suite 400
Philadelphia, PA 19106, USA

www.jkp.com

Library of Congress Cataloging in Publication Data
A CIP catalog record for this book is available from the Library of Congress

British Library Cataloguing in Publication Data
A CIP catalogue record for this book is available from the British Library

ISBN 978 1 84905 148 4
eISBN 978 0 85700 339 3

Printed and bound in Great Britain

With love and appreciation for those who
continue to support us in every way
Mary, Brendan, Eoin and Róisín Dolan
and
P., Oisín and Eoghan Hoban

Contents

About the Authors

Professor Pat Dolan PhD is UNESCO Chair and Director at the Child and Family Research Centre, National University of Ireland (NUI) Galway, Ireland. He is an expert in family support and community-based interventions in helping adolescents, including youth mentoring models. He is co-editor, with John Canavan and John Pinkerton, of *Family Support* and *Family Support as Reflective Practice*, both published by Jessica Kingsley Publishers.

Dr Bernadine Brady PhD is Senior Researcher at the Child and Family Research Centre, NUI Galway, Ireland. She was lead researcher on a major evaluation of the Big Brothers Big Sisters Programme in Ireland, an internationally renowned youth mentoring programme. Her research interests include youth mentoring, civic engagement, family welfare conferencing and children's participation.

Introduction

Since the late 1990s, there has been a growing emphasis on the need for community-based child-centred approaches to promote the welfare of children and young people. A range of localised services has been developed to support children, young people and families in addressing challenges and difficulties in their lives. Although mentoring and befriending programmes have been in existence in the USA for over a century, they have emerged internationally as part of this broader development of services. Such programmes aim to create a private relationship between an adult volunteer and a young person that lasts for a minimum of one year, during which time the pair meets weekly. The 'match' is monitored by a professional caseworker to ensure its safety and progress. The idea is that a friendship will form which will be beneficial to the young person, and help to prevent future difficulties or be a support to them in facing adversity in their lives. The presence of this caring adult is expected to make a difference in the social and emotional development of the young person. Rather than focusing on deficits or what the young person lacks, programmes of this nature emphasise supporting young people to do their best with what they have in the circumstances in which they live.

The purpose of this book is to provide a simple overview of the theory, research and practice of youth mentoring and to highlight in particular how mentoring relationships can enhance the support available to young people. The core argument in the book is that mentoring can be a valuable source of support to young people, particularly those facing adversity or difficulty in their lives. The book aims to provide a thorough understanding of social support as it relates to young people, including the types of support that young people benefit from and the qualities and features of such support and to highlight how mentoring programmes can enhance this. All relationships are complex and the provision of effective support can be difficult. By providing an easily digestible account of the nuances of social support and the potential pitfalls associated with its provision, programme staff, mentors and interested readers will gain an understanding of how their practice can be enhanced. The book also highlights practical ways in which the support available to young people can be assessed, which can help in deciding whether mentoring is appropriate and, for young people who are matched a mentor, whether the relationship is perceived as valuable by them. Furthermore, the book focuses on the nuts and bolts of mentoring, such as recommended practices and research evidence, types of relationships and mentors approach that are more likely to be successful. There is also a focus on issues associated with mentoring in specific contexts such as schools and with particular groups of young people.

What is mentoring?

In the context of this book, 'mentoring' refers to a relationship between a young person (mentee) and an older person (mentor) who is not related to them. There are many definitions of mentoring, all of which are useful. For example, the Youth Mentoring Network in New Zealand provides the following definition:

> The process by which a more experienced, trusted guide forms a relationship with a young person who wants a caring, more experienced person in his/her life, so that the young person is supported in growth towards adulthood and the capacity to make positive social connections and build essential skills is increased. (Dunphy *et al.* 2008, p.9)

This definition emphasises that the relationship is voluntary and reliable and that the young person chooses to become involved. It also highlights that the mentor generally has greater experience than the young person and he or she offers guidance or support that is intended to facilitate the growth and development of the mentee. Other definitions have also acknowledged that there is generally an emotional bond and a sense of trust between the mentor and mentee (DuBois and Karcher 2005). The US National Mentoring Partnership,

MENTOR, describes mentors as 'caring individuals, who along with parents or guardians, provide young people with support, counsel, friendship, reinforcement and a constructive example' (MENTOR/ National Mentoring Partnership 2005, p.11).

Mentoring relationships for young people can be 'informal' or 'formal'. An *informal* or 'natural' mentoring bond is described as a relationship with a non-parental adult (such as a coach, neighbour or teacher) that develops spontaneously and from which the young person receives guidance, encouragement and emotional support (Baker and Maguire 2005). *Formal* or 'planned' mentoring is organised through a mentoring programme and is generally assumed to refer to a one-to-one relationship between an adult volunteer and a young person. Formal mentoring can take place at community and youth clubs, as well as a range of sites including schools and workplaces (DuBois and Karcher 2005). Formal mentoring can take many forms, as outlined in Box I.1.

Box I.1: Types of formal mentoring

One-to-one mentoring: This form of mentoring involves the formation of a relationship between an adult and a young person. Typically, the requirement is that they meet weekly for a minimum of one year.

Group mentoring: Group-based mentoring involves an adult forming a relationship with a group of up to four young people. The mentor commits to meet with the group regularly, the purpose of which may be for fun, teaching or specific activities. The sessions generally have some structure and are led by the mentor.

Team mentoring: This form of mentoring involves several adults mentoring a small group of young people.

Peer mentoring: In peer mentoring, a young person is supported to develop a caring relationship with another youth. Peer mentoring is most likely to occur in school environments. For example, school-based mentoring, as discussed in Chapter 4, involves a mentoring relationship between an older and younger student and generally lasts for the academic year. The role of the older student is to support the younger student in settling into school and dealing with the challenges that children often face in adapting to a new school environment.

Internet mentoring: Internet or e-mentoring involves a one-to-one relationship between an adult and a young person which takes place online. The pair may have some initial face-to-face meetings but continue to communicate via the internet at least once a week. E-mentoring relationships, which are now becoming more popular, often focus on specific goals such as career or academic work.

Source: MENTOR/National Mentoring Partnership (2005)

What is the rationale for mentoring programmes?

A range of reasons for the development of mentoring programmes can be identified and these are now discussed.

Fewer opportunities for informal support between adults and young people

Over the past few decades, the shape and form of 'traditional' family and community life have changed, with significant implications for children and young people's lives. Within the family, children are more likely to live with one parent, while trends such as commuting and increased employment among mothers have reduced the time available for families to spend together. There is a perception that opportunities for informal interaction between adults and young people in school and community have reduced. As a result of these trends, it is argued that young people generally have less access to supportive adults than they may have had in previous generations (Rhodes 2002).

In addition to demographic changes, there is now greater choice and opportunity for young people. Established beliefs and certainties, such as religious values, have been questioned and people have access to a greater range of consumer and media possibilities (Giddens 1991). Some writers, such as Furlong and Cartmel (1997), believe that this weakening of consensus regarding values and the general uncertainty that prevails in modern society have affected young people in particular. They believe that this uncertainty has taken its toll on the mental health of young people, as evidenced in an increase in suicide, attempted suicide, mental disorders and eating disorders. Mentoring programmes aim to provide a safe context for the development of supportive relationships between adults and young people which can act as a resource to young people in navigating the complexities of their lives.

Studies show that social support helps young people cope

A range of research has shown that young people experiencing difficulty are more likely to turn to someone with whom they have a close and trusting relationship, such as a parent, sibling or friend, than to a formal helper such as a social worker or teacher. The availability of support is critical to coping but not all young people have a supportive network on which they can draw to help them to cope. Studies have shown that young people with less social support are at increased risk of problems and that social support contributes to better adjustment generally. For example, Bal *et al.* (2003) concluded from their study of 820 adolescents aged between 12 and 18 years that social support has a major impact on mental health and that adolescents who had experienced a stressful event derived more benefit from the perceived availability of social support.

All young people face stress and difficulty in their lives. Hauser and Bowlds (1990) classify the potential stressors young people face as falling into three categories:

- *Normative events* are experienced by all young people, such as puberty, change of school aged 11–13 and peer pressure. All young people have to confront these issues, usually within a predictable time scale.

- *Non-normative events* concern a smaller group of young people and can occur at any time. These include illness, injury, parental break-up, breakdown in friendships, parental unemployment and bereavement.

- *Daily hassles* are relatively minor in scale but may become significant if there are enough of them or if they combine with normative or non-normative stressors.

The degree to which any of these events will be stressful depends upon the number of events a young person has to contend with, the timing of the events and how normative and non-normative events cluster together. Graber and Brooks-Gunn (1996) emphasise that the young person's ability to cope also depends on the supports or buffers which are available to him or her. Mentoring programmes aim to create a supportive friendship between a young person and an adult in which trust and closeness can develop and the adult can help the young person to cope with whatever normative or non-normative events or daily hassles that he or she experiences.

Studies of 'resilient' young people highlight the importance of mentors

Werner and Smith's (1982) ground-breaking study of young people in Hawaii identified the presence of a consistent care-giver or natural mentor as a key factor in enabling young people to make successful transitions to adulthood, in spite of experiencing significant adversity throughout childhood and adolescence. Further important work by Garmezy (1985) and Rutter and Giller (1983) also drew attention to the presence of at least one non-parental adult who provides consistent support as contributing to the resilience of young people. Rutter (1985) argues that a long-term relationship with mentors can provide a 'steeling mechanism', which helps young people to overcome adversity. Likewise, sociologists Williams and Kornblum (1985) identified the presence of natural mentors as the key difference between youth from disadvantaged communities who are successful and those who are unsuccessful. A range of studies has shown that naturally occurring mentors can serve as important resources in the lives of young people by providing guidance, encouragement and emotional support (Munson et al. 2010; Zimmerman et al. 2002). Formal mentoring programmes aim to foster the development of supportive mentoring relationships for young people who may not have access to natural mentors in their lives.

Drawing on the studies of resilient youth just mentioned, in addition to the broader body of research into youth development, the US National Research Council/Institute of Medicine in 2002 (Eccles and Gootman 2002) identified a set of personal and social assets which increase the healthy development and well-being of adolescents and facilitate successful transition from childhood, through adolescence and into adulthood. These assets are physical development, intellectual development (including critical thinking, school success, life skills), psychological and emotional development (including good coping skills, confidence in one's personal efficacy and pro-social values) and social development (including connectedness to parents, peers and other adults, and sense of social integration). The contexts in which young people live their lives are more likely to provide developmental assets if they have opportunities to experience supportive relationships and good emotional and moral support; exposure to positive morals and values; links with their communities and physical and psychological safety and security (Eccles and Gootman 2002). The authors concluded that community programmes can expand the opportunities for youth to acquire personal and social assets, and that youth who spend time in communities rich in developmental opportunities experience less risk and show higher rates of positive development. As the following quote illustrates, community programmes are not just about tackling problems but set their sights on the 'full potential' of the young person:

> many who study adolescent development and work with young people have increasingly come to believe that being problem-free is not fully prepared. Beyond eliminating problems, one needs skills, knowledge and a variety of other personal and social assets to function well during adolescence and adulthood. Thus a broader, more holistic view of helping youth to realise their full potential is gaining wider credence in the world of policy and practice... (Eccles and Gootman 2002, p.x)

Considered in this context, it is clear that there are many factors associated with positive youth development and that mentoring on its own is not a panacea that can cure the damage caused by a life of disadvantage. Even where positive relationships are facilitated through mentoring programmes, they will represent just one of 'the army' of developmental assets that can support the healthy development of young people.

Mentoring can promote bridging social capital

Social capital refers to the benefits that result from social connections and trust between people (Field 2008; Putnam 2000). The concepts of bridging and bonding social capital in particular have been used in the context of community-based interventions for children and young people. Bonding social capital refers to the close ties and strong localised trust that characterise relationships between people in many communities, while bridging social capital is characterised by weaker ties with people who are not close. The concept of social capital has been drawn on to justify the need for community-based interventions that can strengthen the networks and trust between people in communities (Jack and Jordan 1999). Community-based interventions are generally focused on building up bonding social capital, through creating local supportive networks for people who may be vulnerable. The effects of bonding social capital in a community are generally positive in that people draw on these ties in good times and bad, but they can also be negative by encouraging downward levelling of norms and preventing people from networking with outsiders (Putnam 2000). Woolcock and Narayan (2000) argue that, while localised bonding social capital operates as a defensive strategy against poverty, a shift from 'getting by' to 'getting ahead' requires a shift from bonding to bridging networks.

One may wonder how bonding and bridging social capital connects with social support and youth mentoring. It can be argued that mentoring aims to stimulate 'bridging' social capital, providing a trusting, supportive relationship between a young person and adult, thus opening up the young person's social networks, world views and relationships. The presence of this adult may also influence other family members, such as parents and siblings. In cases where the family world view is closed, for example in relation to education, the mentor may influence the mentees' attitudes through discussing their life experiences. Mentees also have the opportunity to take part in new activities, including sport, cultural and youth groups that otherwise may not be part of their world. Shildrick and MacDonald's study (2008) provided examples of how bridging social capital occurred when natural mentors facilitated young people to broaden their options and enjoy new lifestyles. Likewise, Clayden and Stein's

(2002) study of mentoring for young people leaving care showed that informal relationships with mentors acted, in some cases, to support young people to bypass the negative bonding social capital that can lead them to engage in crime and drug use. Further support for the bridging theory is provided by DuBois and Silverthorn's (2005) nationally representative US study of natural mentors, which found that, compared to mentoring relationships with adults within the family, ties with adults outside the family were more likely to be associated with favourable outcomes in the areas of education and physical health. Education and physical health are areas in which family members often share similar attitudes and behaviours, indicating that adults from outside the family may be better equipped to model and encourage alternative perspectives or approaches for a young person.

Youth mentoring is a flexible, youth-centred model of service provision

As highlighted earlier, the youth mentoring model recognises that children and young people derive support from informal social ties they perceive to be authentic, confidential and meaningful and aims to provide such relationships in the context of a formal programme. Research has shown that young people can be reluctant to share their problems with formal helpers because they fear their problems will not be kept confidential (Hallett et al. 2003). There have been calls for new forms of service provision for children and young people that enable self-expression and are not governed by 'top-down' objectives regarding what children need (Moss and Petrie 2002; Parton 2006). This emphasis on genuine child- and youth-led participation reflects the intention of Article 12 of the United Nations Convention on the Rights of the Child (UNCRC). It can be argued that particular types of mentoring programmes can provide this space for children and young people. Furthermore, in line with Bronfenbrenner's (1979) ecological framework, mentoring can be considered a flexible intervention that is capable of working with the 'whole child' in his or her own environment, culture, context and gender and building on his or her unique strengths. As a social policy intervention, mentoring also has the advantage of being available outside '9 to 5, Monday to Friday' and thus has the capacity to provide support to young people when needed (Brady and Dolan 2007).

In summary, therefore, the rationale for mentoring programmes derives from research and theory which draw attention to the factors that support young people to cope and enjoy a healthy development in society. Because of changes in the nature of family and community lives over recent decades, it is argued that young people don't have as much opportunity to form relationships with adults in their homes and communities as they did previously. Mentoring programmes aim to address this gap by facilitating young people to form supportive relationships with adults in a community setting. Second, there is a large body of research which emphasises the importance of social support in helping young people to cope. Third, studies of young people who have thrived in spite of significant adversity in their lives have highlighted that many drew on the support of a natural mentor. This body of research highlights how access to the support of a non-parental adult can be an important aspect of the lives of resilient youth. Fourth, mentoring is a form of semi-formal service provision, in that it is provided in the context of a professional service but is a flexible, informal form of intervention. Research has shown that young people are more likely to develop trust in and open up to informal supporters than professionals because they are aware that professionals work with them in a paid capacity and may share information with others. However, the literature in relation to mentoring also highlights a number of issues or downsides of youth mentoring, as discussed in the following section.

Are there downsides to mentoring?

The mentoring movement has expanded rapidly and, as a result, critics have argued that the hype that can surround interventions of this nature means that adequate attention may not be paid to the existing natural supports including parents that young people may have in their social networks. Colley (2003) and Philip (2003) argue that mentoring programmes may undermine informal and community-based sources of support. There may be a rush to assume that a mentor is needed in a young person's life, before assessing the supportiveness of his or her existing network (Dolan *et al.* 2008). Some argue that it may be more worthwhile to intervene to enable the young person's established support network to function more effectively (Colley 2003; Philip and Hendry 2000). Cutrona (2000), writing about social support more generally, argues that social network interventions that aim to 'graft' on a new member are less successful than those that work with existing supports. Rhodes (2002) also reminds us that socially supportive relationships can bring conflict as well as support. Colley (2003) questions the argument that mentoring programmes can make young people more resilient, raising the possibility that it is the more resilient young people who seek out natural mentors. There is also concern that young people are left 'high and dry' after their match ends and that they may feel hurt or let down if the mentor chooses to end the relationship. These issues are discussed and addressed throughout the book.

Types of mentoring programmes

The best-known youth mentoring programme in the world is Big Brothers Big Sisters (BBBS) . It was founded in the USA in 1908 and, in the century since its foundation, mentoring programmes have been exported to over 20 countries worldwide and have been adapted and reframed to meet the policy and cultural requirements in different countries. Over the past two decades in particular, there has been a significant expansion in such programmes in the USA, UK and many other countries. According to Philip (2003), the expansion of youth mentoring interventions in the USA during the 1980s had a powerful influence on the development of mentoring in the UK in the 1990s. Mentoring was integrated into a range of government policy initiatives aimed at reducing social exclusion among children, young people and families (Philip and Spratt 2007). Mentoring was introduced as an element of policy provision in sectors such as education, social welfare, employment and training, while a number of flagship services were established to use mentoring models to integrate young people as civic actors. For example, the Connexions service aimed to provide 20,000 young people with a personal mentor, while in Scotland, mentoring was a feature of social inclusion partnerships, which aimed to take a holistic approach to meeting the needs of vulnerable young people. More recently, the Mentoring and

Befriending Foundation was given a significant role in supporting the development of mentoring and befriending across the UK. Philip and Spratt (2007) point out that an infrastructure for the development of mentoring and befriending is clearly in place in the UK and is closely linked to current government policy on youth. There has also been considerable investment in mentoring by private trusts and the wider philanthropic community.

In the UK in particular, a distinction is made between 'befriending' and 'mentoring' programmes. In both approaches, a relationship is supported by a professional agency, but a befriending scheme emphasises the development of a supportive friendship and is not explicitly focused on developing solutions to the young person's problems (Philip and Spratt 2007). 'Low-key' goals may be set after some time but the primary objective is the 'development of a one-to-one relationship between an adult volunteer and a young person... which engages both partners' (Philip and Spratt 2007, p.31). Such schemes are generally run by the voluntary sector and receive referrals from social services. Pawson and Boaz (2004) suggest that mentoring is underpinned by 'befriending', which it then builds on with elements of direction-setting, coaching and sponsorship. Similarly, the Befriending Network Scotland's (BNS) continuum of six types of mentoring and befriending relationships highlights the prominence given to objective-setting as a crucial difference between befriending and mentoring.

Befriending relationships generally don't prioritise the setting or achievement of objectives whereas they define mentoring relationships as having a primary focus on achieving objectives, while the social relationship, if achieved, is incidental (see Box I.2). Programmes at number 5 or 6 on the spectrum in Box I.2 are often targeted at specific policy objectives such as training or crime prevention and may be time limited, whereby the intervention ends when the objectives are deemed to have been met, or by a particular time frame. BNS make the point that these schemes are more suited to people who have a certain level of stability in their lives and can work progressively towards these objectives, whereas more vulnerable or isolated young people are likely to respond better to types 1–3, which emphasise the value of an informal relationship rather than the achievement of specific objectives.

Box I.2: Befriending Network Scotland's befriending/mentoring spectrum

1. *Befriending*: The role of the volunteer is to provide informal social support. The primary objective of the relationship is to form a trusting relationship over time, usually in order to reduce isolation and to provide a relationship where none currently exists. Other outcomes may occur, e.g. a growth in confidence, but these are never set as objectives for the relationship.

2. *Befriending*: The role of the volunteer is to provide informal social support. There may be additional stated objectives at the start of the relationship, e.g. increasing involvement in community activities. The success of the relationship is not dependent on these objectives being achieved, but they are seen as a potential benefit of befriending over time.

3. *Befriending/mentoring*: The role of the volunteer is to provide informal social support and through this supportive relationship to go on to achieve stated objectives, e.g. increasing befriendee/mentee's confidence to enable him or her to do activities independently in the future. The objectives do form a basis of discussion between project, volunteer and befriendee/mentee at an early stage and are reviewed over time.

4. *Mentoring/befriending*: The role of the volunteer is to develop objectives with the befriendee/mentee over time. Initially the role is to develop a relationship through social activities in order to establish a level of trust on which objective-setting can be based. Due to the befriendee's/mentee's changing circumstances, objectives may take time to set and may be low key.

5. *Mentoring*: The role of the volunteer is to work with the befriendee/mentee to meet objectives which are agreed at the start of the relationship. These are achieved through the development of a trusting relationship which involves social elements but which retains a focus on the objectives agreed at the start.

> 6. *Mentoring*: The role of the volunteer is to work with the befriendee/mentee solely on agreed objectives which are clearly stated at the start. Each meeting focuses primarily on achieving the objectives, and the social relationship if achieved is incidental.
>
> *Source*: Befriending Network Scotland (undated, pp.24–25)

Does mentoring make a difference to young people?

DuBois *et al.*'s (2002) meta-analysis of over 55 studies of youth mentoring programmes found that there is a small, but significant, positive effect for mentees in the areas of enhanced psychological, social and academic outcomes, as well as reductions in problem behaviours. There was considerable variation in the effectiveness of different programmes studied. Programmes in which young people had more frequent contact with their mentors and felt emotional closeness to them showed better outcomes. DuBois *et al.* (2002) emphasise that to facilitate attainment of desired outcomes, programmes must adhere closely to recommended guidelines for effective practice. In programmes where youth had more favourable life circumstances and better psychological functioning, the outcomes were also better.

In one of the most high profile studies of youth mentoring ever undertaken, Tierney *et al.* (1995) conducted a large-scale experimental evaluation of the BBBS programme across eight sites in the USA to assess whether mentoring made a tangible difference to the young people's lives. The evaluation found that young people with a mentor were less likely to start using drugs or alcohol; were less likely to hit someone; had improved school attendance and performance; had improved attitudes towards completing schoolwork; and had improved peer and family relationships compared to a control group who did not have a mentor. The study concluded that the organised structure and support of the programme was crucial to its effectiveness. The intensive supervision and support of the mentors by paid staff, which is a feature of the BBBS programme, was especially critical to successful outcomes (Furano *et al.* 1993).

Further analysis of the data from this study was undertaken by Grossman and Rhodes (2002), who found that the outcomes were strongest for young people in matches that lasted for 12 months or more but that young people for whom matches end prematurely (before six months) showed a deterioration in relation to some of the key outcomes (Grossman and Rhodes 2002). This finding highlights the importance of ensuring that matches last for the minimum of 12 months as is the expectation in most mentoring programmes.

Philip and Spratt's (2007) review of published UK research on mentoring and befriending found that young people who developed meaningful relationships with their mentors reported increased confidence, social support and involvement with their communities. For many young people, this relationship was a positive alternative to other relationships with family and professionals and was used as a means of re-negotiating difficult relationships with family and friends. Young people with positive mentoring relationships were more likely to return to education and do well than those whose relationships failed. They found that building and sustaining mentoring interventions takes time, persistence and skill.

Programmes that were well planned, with clear processes for recruitment, training and support both to mentors and young people, were more likely to offer the potential for meaningful mentoring to develop (Philip and Spratt 2007, p.6). On the negative side, they found that endings could be problematic, even where properly planned. Recruitment of mentors, particularly male, was a difficult issue while 'large numbers of those involved in mentoring projects' failed to develop relationships at all (p.46).

Schemes that target young people at risk of disengaging or already disengaged from formal schemes of education, training or employment have been described as 'engagement mentoring' (Colley 2003, p.18). Pawson and Boaz (2004) and Colley (2003) draw attention to the fact that engagement mentoring schemes, which are a key component of UK social inclusion policies, are asking a lot from mentors, expecting them to work with very disaffected young people to 'turn their lives around'. Colley's (2003) study of engagement mentoring schemes found that, when young people were allowed to negotiate mentoring relationships on the basis of their own needs and concerns, they usually perceived mentoring in a highly positive way and could identify important benefits from the process (p.162). However, Colley found that a focus on hard outcomes in these 'engagement mentoring' schemes undermined the gains that were made in the areas of confidence, outlook and aspirations. She argues that mentors are capable of achieving private goals and, ironically, if they are left alone to do this, these gains will aggregate into public goals but the control exercised by formal mentoring programmes often did not allow this. Similarly, Philip and Spratt (2007) describe how the ability of the Connexions service to meet the needs of its vulnerable target group was undermined by favouring 'employability' over the meeting of other needs such as housing or relationships. Overall, the research suggests that the prioritisation of official outcomes over the individual needs of the mentees was harmful to efforts on the parts of young people and mentors to develop trusting relationships and undermined potential gains (Colley 2003; Meier 2008; Philip and Spratt 2007).

In summary, therefore, mentoring programmes can achieve modest gains in outcomes for young people. While there is now greater knowledge regarding what types of mentoring work, in what contexts and for whom, academics argue that the expansion of youth mentoring initiatives both in the USA and UK has outpaced evidence of its effectiveness (DuBois and Rhodes 2006; Philip and Spratt 2007). The most successful programmes are those that work with young people who experience disadvantage and prioritise the 'friendship factor' rather than the harder indicators such as employment and reduced drug and alcohol use. There has been a tendency to overstate the potential of youth mentoring programmes to change young people's lives. For example, George Bush said in his 2001 inaugural address that 'some needs and hurts are so deep they will only respond to a mentor's touch or a pastor's prayer' (Rhodes 2002, p.114). Rhodes points out that the research indicates that the deepest needs and hurts are unlikely to respond to a mentor's touch alone and emphasises that mentoring cannot make up for years of accumulated failure in important influences such as the educational system, family and the economy. In sum, a young person's problems do not occur in isolation and cannot be cured in an isolated mentoring relationship.

Overview of the book's contents

As we have just seen, research shows that some types of mentoring are more effective than others. This book argues that the youth mentoring model can be a valuable intervention for young people. The emphasis is on enhancing the support available to young people, in the belief that this support acts as a buffer to protect them against risk and enable their coping. By focusing on the creation and maintenance of a relationship that the young person perceives as supportive, programmes can facilitate young people to be in charge of their own direction in life and to have a confidential space in which they can pursue their interests. However, mentoring is not a panacea and it will not work for all young people. There will be cases where matches end early and the young person may feel let down and disappointed. As with all human relationships, there is potential for upset as well as positive outcomes and these must be clearly acknowledged.

This model of mentoring that is advocated in this book can be considered as a positive youth development approach in that it is about enhancing the well-being of the young person, rather than identifying top-down indicators in relation to education or crime prevention. The programme should be child and youth centred and led, guided by rigorous programme practices, involve parents and work with children and young people in the context of their lives. The model emphasises the development of a supportive friendship. While goals may be set, this should not happen until after the friendship is firmly established, so it should be 'friendship first – future fixing second'.

A key message in this book is that mentoring should only be considered for young people who would benefit from support. As part of assessing the child's suitability for the programme, it is crucial to assess his or her social support network to identify where sources of help are present. Also, it is argued that because the ending of the relationship may be stressful for the young person, it is valuable to look at how the supports in the young person's own ecology can be mobilised in the longer term.

Following this Introduction, Chapter 1 explores the importance of support for young people. The chapter illustrates the types of support that young people can benefit from, the qualities and characteristics of supportive relationships and the issues associated with their establishment and maintenance. Throughout the chapter, we look at the ways in which practical help, emotional sustenance, advice and esteem support can be provided in mentoring relationships, the importance of reciprocity and the outcomes that can accrue from the provision of support. Mentoring will not be suitable for all young people and many may have sufficient support in their lives. It is good practice for a practitioner to assess the support network in a young person's life as a means of understanding if a mentor is needed. Thus, in Chapter 2, two tools for gauging the support networks of young people are introduced and described as part of the assessment process.

Having established how mentoring relationships can be supportive, the book then moves on to look at specific contexts in which mentoring can be provided – including community settings, schools and for vulnerable groups. Chapter 3 provides an overview of the factors that are associated with good practice in mentoring programmes. These include the need for rigorous assessment and monitoring of matches, attention to the recruitment of male volunteers and the need for ongoing activities for mentors and young people. Chapter 4 highlights the potential for both adult–youth and peer mentoring in school contexts. Such programmes can support young people at the critical juncture of starting secondary school and provide opportunities for older youth to develop mentoring skills. In Chapter 5, we look at mentoring models for specific populations of young people, including young people leaving care, those with disabilities, refugee and asylum-seeking young people and youth with mental health issues. Also in this chapter we focus on the potential of intergenerational mentoring and issues relating to mentoring in the context of youth justice services. The Conclusion revisits key messages from the book and considers social support and youth mentoring from a rights-based perspective.

References

Baker, D.B. and Maguire, C.P. (2005) 'Mentoring in Historical Perspective.' In D.L. DuBois and M.J. Karcher (eds) *Handbook of Youth Mentoring*. Thousand Oaks, CA: Sage Publications.

Bal, S., Crombez, G., Van Oost, P. and Debourdeaudhuij, I. (2003) 'The role of social support in well-being and coping with self-reported stressful events in adolescents.' *Child Abuse and Neglect 27*, 12, 1377–1395.

Befriending Network Scotland (undated) *The Befriending and Mentoring Evaluation Toolkit.* Edinburgh: BNS. Available at www.befriending.co.uk/befriendingpublications.php, accessed on 18 July 2011.

Brady, B. and Dolan, P. (2007) 'Youth mentoring in Ireland: Weighing up the benefits and challenges.' *Youth Studies Ireland 2*, 1, 3–16.

Bronfenbrenner, U. (1979) *The Ecology of Human Development: Experiments by Nature and Design.* Cambridge, MA: Harvard University Press.

Clayden, J. and Stein, M. (2002) *Mentoring for Care Leavers: Evaluation Report.* London: The Prince's Trust.

Colley, H. (2003) *Mentoring for Social Inclusion.* London: Routledge Falmer.

Cutrona, C.E. (2000) 'Social Support Principles for Strengthening Families.' In J. Canavan, P. Dolan and J. Pinkerton (eds) *Family Support: Direction from Diversity.* London: Jessica Kingsley Publishers.

Dolan, P., Canavan, J. and Brady, B. (2008) 'Youth mentoring and the parent–young person relationship: Considerations for research and practice.' *Youth and Policy 99*, Spring, 13–17.

DuBois, D.L. and Karcher, M.J. (2005) 'Youth Mentoring: Theory, Research and Practice.' In D.L. DuBois and M.J. Karcher (eds) *Handbook of Youth Mentoring.* Thousand Oaks, CA: Sage Publications.

DuBois, D.L. and Rhodes, J.E. (2006) 'Introduction to the Special Issue: Youth mentoring: bridging science with practice.' *Journal of Community Psychology 34*, 6, 647–655.

DuBois, D.L. and Silverthorn, N. (2005) 'Characteristics of natural mentoring relationships and adolescent adjustment: Evidence from a national study.' *Journal of Primary Prevention 26*, 2, 69–92.

DuBois, D.L., Holloway, B.E., Valentine, J.C. and Cooper, H. (2002) 'Effectiveness of mentoring programs for youth: A meta-analytic review.' *American Journal of Community Psychology 30*, 2, 157–197.

Dunphy, A., Gavin, B., Solomon, F., Stewart, C., Collins, E. and Grant, A. (2008) *Guide to Effective Practice in Youth Mentoring New Zealand.* Henderson, Auckland: Youth Mentoring Network. Available at www.youthmentoring.org.nz/tools/index.cfm, accessed on 26 May 2010.

Eccles, J. and Gootman, J. (2002) *Community Programs to Promote Youth Development.* Washington, DC: National Academy Press.

Field, J. (2008) *Social Capital* (2nd edition). Abingdon: Routledge.

Furano, K., Roaf, P.A, Styles, M.B and Branch, A.Y. (1993) *Big Brothers Big Sisters: A Study of Program Practices.* Philadelphia, PA: Public/Private Ventures.

Furlong, A. and Cartmel, F. (1997) *Young People and Social Change: Individualisation and Risk in Late Modernity.* Buckingham: Open University Press.

Garmezy, N. (1985) 'Stress-resistant children: The search for protective factors.' In J.E. Stevenson (ed.) *Recent Research in Developmental Psychopathology (Journal of Child Psychology and Psychiatry 4).* Oxford: Pergamon Press.

Giddens, A. (1991) *Modernity and Self-identity.* Cambridge: Polity Press.

Graber, J.A. and Brooks-Gunn, J. (1996) 'Transitions and turning points: Navigating the passage from childhood through adolescence.' *Developmental Psychology 32*, 768–776.

Grossman, J.B. and Rhodes, J.E. (2002) 'The test of time: Predictors and effects of duration in youth mentoring relationships.' *American Journal of Community Psychology 30*, 2, 199–219.

Hallett, C., Murray, C. and Punch, S. (2003) 'Young people and welfare: Negotiating pathways.' In C. Hallett and A. Prout (eds) *Hearing the Voices of Children: Social Policy for a New Century.* London: Routledge Falmer.

Hauser, S. and Bowlds, M. (1990) 'Stress, Coping and Adaptation.' In S.S. Feldman and G.R. Elliott (eds) *At the Threshold, the Developing Adolescent.* Cambridge, MA: Harvard University Press.

Jack, G. and Jordan, B. (1999) 'Social capital and child welfare.' *Children and Society 13*, 242–256.

Meier, R. (2008) *Youth Mentoring: A Good Thing?* London: Centre for Policy Studies.

MENTOR/National Mentoring Partnership (2005) *How to Build a Successful Mentoring Program Using the Elements of Effective Practice: A Step by Step Toolkit for Program Managers.* Alexandria, VA: MENTOR/National Mentoring Partnership.

Moss, P. and Petrie, P. (2002) *From Children's Services to Children's Spaces: Public Policy, Children and Childhood.* London: Routledge Falmer.

Munson, M.R., Smalling, S.E., Spencer, R., Scott, L.D. and Tracy, E.M. (2010) 'A steady presence in the midst of change: Non-kin natural mentors in the lives of older youth exiting foster care.' *Children and Youth Services Review 32*, 4, 527–535.

Parton, N. (2006) *Safeguarding Childhood: Early Intervention and Surveillance in a Late Modern Society.* Basingstoke: Palgrave Macmillan.

Pawson, R. and Boaz, A. (2004) *Methods Briefing 3: Evidence-based Policy, Theory-based Synthesis, Practice-based Reviews.* Leeds: ESRC. Available at www.ccrs.ac.uk/methods/publications/documents/pawson.pdf, accessed on 14 September 2010.

Philip, K. (2003) 'Youth mentoring: The American dream comes to the UK?' *British Journal of Guidance and Counselling 31*, 1, 101–112.

Philip, K. and Hendry, L.B. (2000) 'Making sense of mentoring or mentoring making sense? Reflections on the mentoring process by adult mentors with young people.' *Journal of Community and Applied Social Psychology 10*, 3, 211–223.

Philip, K. and Spratt, J. (2007) *A Synthesis of Published Research on Mentoring and Befriending.* Manchester: Mentoring and Befriending Foundation.

Putnam, R.D. (2000) *Bowling Alone: The Collapse and Revival of American Community.* New York: Simon & Schuster.

Rhodes, J.E. (2002) *Stand By Me: The Risks and Rewards of Mentoring Today's Youth.* Cambridge, MA: Harvard University Press.

Rutter, M. (1985) 'Resilience in the face of adversity: Protective factors and resistance to psychiatric disorders.' *British Journal of Psychiatry 147*, 589–611.

Rutter, M. and Giller, H. (1983) *Juvenile Delinquency: Trends and Perspectives.* New York: Guilford Press.

Shildrick, T.A. and MacDonald, R. (2008) 'Understanding youth exclusion: Critical moments, social networks and social capital.' *Youth and Policy 99*, 46–64.

Tierney. J., Grossman, J. and Resch, N. (1995) *Making a Difference: An Impact Study of Big Brothers Big Sisters of America.* Philadelphia, PA: Public/Private Ventures.

Werner, E.E. and Smith, R.S. (1982) *Vulnerable but Invincible: A Study of Resilient Children.* New York: McGraw-Hill.

Williams, T.M. and Kornblum, W. (1985) *Growing Up Poor.* Lexington, MA: D.C. Heath and Co.

Woolcock, M. and Narayan, D. (2000) 'Social capital: Implications for development theory, research, and policy.' *World Bank Research Observer 15*, 2, 225.

Zimmerman, M.A., Bingenheimer, J.B. and Notaro, P.C. (2002) 'Natural mentors and adolescent resiliency: A study with urban youth.' *American Journal of Community Psychology 30*, 2, 221–243.

Chapter 1

Understanding Social Support and Its Role in Youth Mentoring

Introduction

In this chapter we explore the concept of social support and how it can play a key role both in the lives of youth and in the context of mentoring programmes. The benefits and limitations of social networks as sources of help are unpacked, including a 'run-through' on what is known as important and central in enabling the coping capacity of young people in times of stress. More positively, how social support networks can enhance the plight of youth within family, school, community and mentoring contexts are considered. The chapter starts with a definition of social support emphasising its central importance in the lives of youth, and an outline of its key characteristics including types, quantity and qualities. However, not all support that youth donate or receive is positive and occasionally social networks are a cause of rather than a cure for stress. So the limitations of social support are also considered. Finally, sample methods for enlisting better social support for young people including 'support banking' and a 'convoy model' are described.

What is social support?

Just like adults and younger children, youth need social support from others as a central resource in their lives. Generally, social support means the acts we perform in order to give or get help and relates to those which reduce stress and assist coping in life. It constitutes everything from words and actions to feelings that enable support and can differ depending on a person's problems and circumstances. There is consensus among many writers and researchers that fully understanding social support can be difficult, and Veiel and Baumann (1992), from their comprehensive review of the literature, indicate that establishing one clear definition of social support is challenging. More simply, there are many definitions for social support and all of them good, but they are not the same or interchangeable. However, Cutrona in her review of definitions and in seeking to answer the simple yet complex question, 'What is social support?' defines it very neatly as 'acts that demonstrate responsivity to another's needs' (1996, p.17). For our purposes in this book we are using this simple and succinct definition by Carolyn Cutrona.

Receiving social support does far more than provide us with a sense of feeling good. Effective social supporters provide us with help and collectively act as 'safeguards to stress'. This function of social support 'as a buffer to stress' has been well established within the research literature and it is noteworthy that it is one of the more proven theories within the social sciences. The availability of social support enhances mental health and strengthens ability to cope in a crisis. More specifically, having social support available assists youth's self-esteem and self-efficacy. In very tangible terms it can also play a key role in protecting youth at risk whereby positive and accessible social support networks have been identified as offering protection (Thompson 1995). Similarly, for some adolescents effective social support networks can be central in that help from a reliable alliance can help avert suicidal ideation and acts.

Social support and social networks for youth – amounts of help vs. sources of help

As indicated above, at a broad base social support relates to acts of assistance between people and typically involves a donor (a person who provides the support) and a recipient (he or she who benefits). In a youth mentoring relationship the roles of both parties are obvious in this regard, although the mutual benefit to mentor and mentee should not go unnoticed. For any of us in need of help (regardless of age) the pool of people whom we turn to represents our sources of support and can be defined as a social network. This set of people is usually made up of family (either nuclear or extended), friends, neighbours and work or school colleagues, and can also include professionals. Importantly, whereas the size of a network may be emphasised, it does not necessarily mean that the bigger the network the greater the support that will follow. So while a young person might have a very small network of say four or five people, he or she may still get an abundance of help. Conversely, another young person may nominate a large set of people in his or her network but may only be able to harvest small amounts of assistance (Cutrona 2000). This fact in itself is important in working with youth. Professionals such as youth workers often assume that if a young person can nominate lots of friendships and social contacts that support is plentiful. Such a belief is mythical. Dolan (2010) suggests that an association between size and support levels in networks should not be assumed in practice. If you simply increase the size of a young person's network, it does not necessarily mean he or she will receive more support or perceive the presence of personal resources.

Informal support and the role of a reliable alliance for youth

Informal sources of social support (e.g. family and friends) represent those who give help freely, and are generally preferable for young people because they are available every day and all day, and are a more natural source of help. They are automatically where young people go for help. Importantly, receiving help from sources such as family and friends is less stigmatising and reduces a young person's sense of being beholden; it also stems a belief that they need 'professional help', which in itself is very important to young people. However, that is not to say that professionals such as teachers and youth workers do not have a key role. It should be remembered that in certain contexts support from formal sources (professionals) are preferred. For example, a young person with a troublesome loose tooth would be better off having a dentist do the extraction rather than a willing friend using the string and door handle technique.

While we all use different sources in our networks for differing purposes and at various points in our lives, usually at least one person who is a 'reliable alliance' may be of central importance. This applies in exactly the same way during the adolescent years. This person (or perhaps two or three people) is typically someone with whom we have an intimate relationship and can be turned to for help, during everyday living and in a crisis. For most youth this reliable alliance is a parent or parents and/or an intimate friend or small set of friends. Occasionally this closeness even may form a lifelong connection for youth. This relationship(s) is key to a young person's capacity to cope, and while many young people may nominate friends, few may describe these ties as close. However, many experts on social support rightfully also caution against having all relationship needs provided by one person. This is like a young person having all his or her 'eggs in one basket'. If this is the sole source of help for a young person and if the relationship ends, for example the supporter dies or there is a breakdown in the relationship, the youth can find him- or herself stranded with no other source of help. Similarly for youth who rely solely on family as their support source: if they fall out with one person in their family it sometimes means that they fall out with all their family, which can have very obvious negative effects. Most youth like choice for support and to have the luxury of family and friendships within their networks. This means that they can keep both parties separate and essentially 'shop around' between sources for help as needed.

Box 1.1: Some key learning points

1. Social support for youth is the bread and butter of relationships.

2. Informal (non-paid) sources of social support are the most valuable resource to young people.

3. Larger social networks do not automatically bring greater support for youth and occasionally just a few supporters can be key and provide plentiful help.

Types of social support that network memberships provide to young people

Apart from the matter of who gives help to youth, the equally key issue of what types of assistance is offered needs to be considered. Here we explore the four main kinds of social support youth utilise and then the accompanying four key qualities that act as lynchpins in their proactive social network relationships. Whereas for many years the literature has described types of support in many differing forms, the four most common types (and the ones we are highlighting in this book) are:

1. concrete support

2. emotional support

3. support through advice

4. esteem support.

While some writers, such as Tracy and Whittaker (1990), have focused attention on the first three forms of support identified above, Weiss (1974), who in the early 1970s originally classified types of social support, included esteem support as an important type in its own right. We now consider each of these types of social support separately and in the context of mentoring before going on to look at the 'interplay' of the four forms of support.

Concrete support during adolescence

Concrete support is clearly visible and relates to practical forms of help such as a young person loaning a book or money to a schoolmate, or helping a friend tidy out a garage. Sometimes referred to as 'tangible support', concrete help can be measured as physical acts of helping between a young person and his or her social network membership, which includes acts of assistance on his or her part. As many parents of teenagers can attest, the practical support needs of young people are manifold and include financial and time costs varying from multiple lifts to and from events, to clothes, school and leisure pursuit expenses. For many youth, of all the forms of support concrete help is often assumed as available (although still valued). However, for youth experiencing adversity, most notably poverty, such help unfortunately may not be as automatically available. One could argue that young people's need for practical support is often overlooked by professionals. For example, sometimes a youth may only need tangible help, such as the price of a pair of football boots, the purchase of which will enable the young person to continue to play competitive sports.

A very obvious and physical way that mentors provide practical support to young people and their parents lies in the simple task of their bringing the young people out of the home and introducing them to new places, people and activities. For example, in cases where a family is quite large, the parent(s) are unlikely to have time to bring the young person to the places he or she would wish to go. So, practically, mentors often provide opportunities to young people to go places that they would not be able to go to independently. Such tangible help from mentors also enables social participation or integration in supportive relationships whereby the mentee benefits from meeting others, companionship and sharing leisure activities. This is particularly important for youth who have a tendency towards introversion, with their mentoring relationship providing basic opportunities to be more sociable. Concrete support can be also viewed as a form of bridging social capital (Putnam 2000) wherein young people are helped to make use of social and community resources and to take advantage of opportunities emanating from the mentor's own social networks and connections.

Case example 1.1: John (14 years), budding musician

John mixes and records music off the deck in a local youth café and then send the tracks to his mentor's laptop. John's mentor in turn sends the mixed new version of the music to John's phone. He then puts the music up on YouTube and distributes this to a set of friends. Recently John got a reference email about one of his songs and to his delight found the song got 16,000 listens, which he simply describes as 'brilliant'. In this example the practical support offered by John's mentor in terms of technical help was key to John furthering this hobby.

Emotional support for youth

Emotional support during adolescence is a more sensitive form of help and typically relates to feelings and involves intimate relationships. Usually emotional help is about being there for people we feel close to, listening to them if they are upset and offering unconditional love. Whereas youth have similar emotional needs to adults or younger children, given the sometimes tumultuous nature of the teenage experience, there are specific levels of support required. The generalisation that teenage boys like doing and are less inclined to discuss feelings than girls may be contested; nevertheless, in times of stress having strong emotional support during adolescence is crucial. In fact, it is often only when warmth from others is lacking that youth become aware of their feelings and emotional needs. More simply, emotional support can be deemed to be information that leads people to believe they are cared for and is considered one of the most valuable forms of support. Crucially, emotional support has potential value in all situations in life.

Within youth mentoring relationships, mentors often refer to their conversations with their 'little'[1] as an important part of the relationship, and are typically very happy to take the lead from young people regarding what they wish to discuss. Empathy, which is demonstrated by understanding another person's frame of reference and emotional experience, is key to mentoring and emotional support.

Importantly, emotional support needs to be given regularly and in everyday living contexts as well as when young people are distressed. While friends, unlike parents, may not explicitly provide emotional support to other youth they often do so implicitly. Many young people show emotional solidarity to friends by their presence or subtle acts of support. For example, a young person who experiences bullying at school may be protected merely by the physical presence of friends at particular times of vulnerability.

Mentors often help young people to deal with emotions which enables them to interact more effectively with others and to deal with negative situations. Youth, like adults, deal with stress in different ways. Support that does not match an individual young person's style of coping will not be effective. For some young people, particularly

---

1   The term 'little' is commonly used to describe a mentee, while a mentor can be referred to as 'big'.

girls, talking about the stress in their lives is their preferred way of coping, whereas for others acting on issues is more important.

Case example 1.2: Marion (12 years), coping with being bullied

Marion was going through a rough patch at the time of her parents' marriage break-up and was being bullied in school. No matter what her parents did to help, it was making it worse in Marion's eyes. Her adult mentor was of great help. She spent many hours just listening to and reassuring Marian. Importantly she repeatedly reminded Marion that she did not have to put up with such bullying. Over time the bullying was addressed and Marion ascribes this to the support she got from her mentor who was there for her to listen to her when she really needed it.

Emotional support can therefore take different forms, including the mentor listening to and empathising with the young person and acting as a 'sounding board' for typical daily events as well as sudden challenges. Some youth may openly converse about personal issues and seek direct support in addressing them, while others may not have personal difficulties in their lives and need a more generic form of ongoing emotional sustenance from their mentor.

Advising youth and providing guidance

Advice or information support to youth, which is also often referred to as 'guidance support', relates to helping someone with a decision or giving him or her information on how best to complete a task. For instance, where a young person is deciding to apply for a job or college placement, he or she will benefit from a friend who advises on the decision to firstly apply, and then by offering guidance on interview preparation and skills. However, providing advice support can be tricky, particularly if the young person just wants verbal endorsement for a bad decision he or she has already made. Parents have to be careful in offering advice to their adolescent offspring, in particular where the young person may perceive the advice on offer as a diktat from their mother and/or father on what is expected and seen as the right course of action. Additionally, there are often kernel points and events where youth will require advice or guidance. Within a youth mentoring relationship, guidance is likely to be more readily accepted if it is provided in a way that does not make the recipient feel belittled by the experience. Advice is something that is accepted more easily when the relationship is well established, and where the advice can form part of a normal conversation.

Case example 1.3: Shirish (15 years) and his struggle with literacy

Shirish is described by his mentor as reluctant to take guidance or instruction and tends not to want to do anything that he 'cannot be the best at'. As a result, Shirish's literacy skills were poor and he would not accept extra tuition at school. Shirish's mentor reassured him that he didn't know everything and asked Shirish to advise him on how to use Facebook. When Tom realised he could advise his mentor, he began to seek and accept advice on his literacy issue.

Holding young people in high esteem

Although not as obvious as concrete, emotional or advice support, esteem support relates to how others rate and inform youth in respect of their worth and competency. It is not about self-esteem but relates to the value others have of a young person. During adolescence having a sense of parity of regard with and from others is key. Being held in positive esteem by other adults and or other youth reinforces a young person's positive feelings of worth. Essentially, if others have belief in the skills of a young person this enables him or her to achieve and succeed. Too often youth are only valued for their prowess in sport or school and other capacities, such as being an honourable or caring person, go unnoticed or unappreciated. Young people can be strong social civic actors supporting others in their family and community but not receive esteem recognition.

The power of youth mentoring has particular currency for esteem support as it connects to how young people can start to see themselves through the eyes of others. Simply, if youth are viewed positively by their mentor, they start to see themselves more positively, which can directly assist their identity development. The fact that mentors value their mentees by giving freely of their time in itself provides an important positive message to the young people.

Case example 1.4: Anna (12 years), playing soccer

Anna was very socially isolated in school and had very few friends who lived near her. She was particularly good at soccer and her mentor practised with her, reminding Anna of how good a goalkeeper she was. When she was accepted for the under 14s school team, Anna was particularly thrilled that her mentor took time off work to come and see her play. This was a huge positive esteem 'injection' for Anna as her teammates were also delighted with the support of the mentor. Over time Anna went on to develop close friendships with some of her teammates.

Further considerations regarding types of support

While the four types of support described here are needed and are valuable to youth in different situations, Cutrona (2000) suggests that emotional support may be of most importance, because it has currency in almost all situations. This has particular relevance to mentoring. There may be times that practical support is sought, but a young person is just offered a kind word in its place from his or her mentor. While this is not what was asked for, it is still important as the young person is reassured that support is available. However, if a youth is very upset, needing reassurance, and seeks emotional support from the same mentor, practical support, although offered with good intent, will not suffice at all. The young person is likely to interpret the mentor's action as cold and uncaring. Young people are discerning about whom they turn to for emotional support. While they will access practical help and advice from a range of network sources, there are a select few to whom they will revert for emotional support and this may or may not include their mentor. For example, a young person may access practical help from a range of friends in order to do well in school, but only approach one or two of them (and possibly the mentor) with regard to a particular personal problem.

Advice support is also a delicate form of support to provide and can be hard to receive, as we tend to 'shop around' for this type of support. For instance, youth may seek advice support only from a donor who they think will give them the response they want to hear, so mentors have to be conscious of this possibility. Additionally, mental health issues may influence a youth's ability to receive advice no matter how tactfully it is delivered or how well it is intended on the part of the mentor. Thus, giving advice can be risky for all parties involved, and Cutrona (2000) warns against being too free with advice support, particularly in close relationships. She further advises that 'if individuals are uncertain about what type of support to offer, they should give emotional support' (p.109).

Giving 'TEA' to youth – a simple way to think about support typology

So, social support for youth can come in four forms: tangible assistance, emotional help, the positive esteem of others or advice. However, for the purpose of simplicity it may be useful to think of support as equating with having a cup of 'TEA' (as having tea with someone is often seen as supportive) which includes **T**angible, **E**motional, **E**steem and **A**dvice support. This is illustrated in Figure 1.1. TEA is also represented as buoyant and non-static with an element of balance. The reason for this is that, in general, young people need all forms of support to thrive so, for example, one young girl living in a rural area might have lots of emotional support (E) from loved ones but her specific need might be for tangible (T) help in the form of someone to provide a lift to the local village or school. Similarly the presence of buoyancy or capacity to seek differing forms of support as the situation dictates is also crucial. For instance, whereas a young person needs emotional support (E) at the very immediate time of a parent suddenly passing away, later (within a day or so) the need might be for advice (A) in relation to helping the remaining grieving parent organise the funeral arrangements.

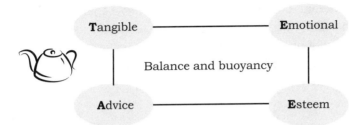

TEA as a model for types of social support

Figure 1.1 TEA – ensuring balance and buoyancy in differing forms of social support

The importance of perceived support

The support perceived by youth as available is of equal importance (if not more important) than the actual support they receive. It is important to remember that when young people believe there are others who would support them, even when this is not so, they may still be strengthened by this false belief. On the other hand, as is often the case among youth who experience adversity, those who hold a perception that nobody is willing or interested in supporting them may never access or mobilise the actual supply of help on hand. This has a key implication for mentoring relationships in that where a young person connects well with his or her mentor, the mere fact of the existence of the relationship in itself may bring perceived benefits which contain value. So you get a double positive effect. First, the actual support on offer from the mentor in real terms can bring dividends and the potential or expected benefits even where they are not accessed also have importance. Unfortunately, the flip or negative side to this equation also applies. Where the young person retains a false perception of low availability or willingness by a mentor to help, it may be difficult to change this view. In fact, in such circumstances actual help offered across the TEA spectrum may go unnoticed.

Additionally, it may well be that those young people who see themselves as able to access help may have good relationship skills in the first place, and it is this capacity which helps them to become more 'supportable'. Conversely, some other youth, because of their perceived feelings of low worth, can see themselves as restricted to only seeking help from formal agencies, such as social work or the police, despite the possible wider availability of informal social support, including that of a mentor. So it is important to emphasise that the enlisting of social support is dependent on factors within the person, including self-perception, as well as external influences in his or her social environment.

Box 1.2: Some key learning points

1. Youth need a variety of types of support in their lives.

2. Emotional support from others can be essential for young people.

3. Providing advice can be tricky.

4. The provision of esteem support can feature prominently in good relationships including that of support from a mentor.

Quality of social support

Apart from types and amounts of social support, the quality of the actual support young people receive is also important. Help that is offered begrudgingly or with a personal cost to young people and/or their family is by its nature a poor quality of support. If as a result of accessing help a young person feels beholden to someone else and/or stressed, then the personal costs that accrue can easily outweigh the benefits received. From the perspective of social support from a mentor, robust screening for suitability of mentors and subsequent monitoring of the quality of matches are key in order to protect against such episodes of toxic support provision. Thus, social support quality can be considered across four dimensions as listed below:

- closeness
- reciprocity
- admonishment (which is non-criticising)
- durability.

These domains are now considered generally and specifically in the context of mentoring.

Closeness

Closeness is an important dimension of social support. As Cutrona (1996) suggests, the development of close ties 'is hard to imagine in the absence of a consistent exchange of supportive acts' (p.13). Closeness to network members relates to the extent to which young people retain feelings of ease, comfort and familiarity with and towards those in their social network. The closer that they feel to someone, the more likely they will be to mobilise support and not perceive themselves to be a burden. Generally, youth tend to have feelings of closeness towards loved ones, for example parents, near family members or long-established friends. Importantly, whereas young people tend to be close to a number of people in their lives, there are few people and perhaps sometimes only one person with whom they are intimately close. This person may be a key source of social support and typically would be someone with whom youth would share their most personal needs, for example a deep concern about their feelings of depression. Such an ally is usually classified as a 'confidante'. There is of course a difference between closeness and intimacy and professionals need to be wary of reading too much into a young person speaking of having a lot of close allies. In sum, whereas young people may be close to many they are only intimate with a few and sometimes nobody. Youth mentoring is a befriending programme and, though it is powerful in its potential and in what it delivers, assumptions should not be made in terms of closeness. The role of the mentor is not to supplant parents in terms of closeness and, given mentoring is time limited, although it is likely to be a source of closeness to the mentee, it is unlikely to become an 'intimate bond'. Having said this, an appropriate level of closeness between the mentor and mentee is a sign of the success of the match and an indicator of the availability or likelihood of support for the young person.

:ciprocity

In everyday life, young people often exchange support automatically with others, for example week in week out working with a close friend on completing homework from school. Thus reciprocal support applies to the extent to which favours provided to others can be returned. Reciprocity also relates to the extent to which youth feel there is a balance of give and take within social relationships. Ideally, young people should be seeking to have regular and equitable exchanges of support with social contacts. A give and take balance ensures that over time youth are not beholden to others and brings them personal status – others grow to value them as support providers as well as recipients of help. For example, in mentoring relationships young people can give support to as well as receive support from their mentor.

However, it is important to remember that if there is an imbalance in the provision of support, the relationship may not last over time. Again in a mentoring context, if a youth is constantly over-seeking support and help from the mentor, or the mentor is not open to the young person's potential to reciprocate, the relationship may suffer. In sum the presence of reciprocity is a hallmark of genuinely supportive relationships.

Admonishment (non-criticising)

A third core quality of social support relates to admonishment. Criticism in social support focuses on the extent to which a social supporter criticises a young person in a way that makes him or her feel bad or inadequate. The existence of high rates of disparagement from network members is obviously undesirable and can have the effect of furthering a young person's belief that they are no good. People don't want to have others around who continuously undermine their self-esteem. Youth are less likely to approach a person for support if they believe that they will receive criticism as part of the cost of accessing that help.

Many mentees experience ongoing negative criticism from other sources, often including family members. Thus it is important that the mentor–mentee bond is non-criticising and, if there is any challenging of the young person, that it is undertaken in a sensitive and caring fashion. A healthy function of youth mentoring by older peers or adults would be where a criticism is utilised positively, in a way that a young person can deal with and benefit from. However, it should be noted that while some constructive criticism is fine, in general the mentor should avoid being critical of his or her mentee.

Durability

Social support for youth is dependent on consistency and availability. Young people need to be reasonably sure that if they seek support from another person, there is a reasonable chance that the required support will be offered. A person who is dependable in this way is often referred to by the recipient youth as being 'a rock of support' to them. But such supporters need to be available. For example, if a young person needs a lift to attend a social outing and an aunt is willing to help, because she lives far away such support is inaccessible. Similarly, if young people seek support from a person whom they have not seen or had any contact with for many years, contacting the person 'out of the blue' would be inappropriate and could possibly lead to disappointment for the young support seeker. Likewise, if a young person has only known someone for a very short length of time and seeks support, that person may be wary because the relationship is new and not be ready yet to offer support.

Like a good bus service, which is dependable and regular, mentors should see their mentees week in week out and offer consistent help. If over time a young person's sense of ease and assuredness with the mentor grows it is likely that he or she will be more inclined to seek help from the mentor and to value the mentor's support. Apart from building the relationship regular contact also instils a sense for the mentee that the mentor is dependable.

CARD as a method for ensuring good quality support for young people

Just as TEA was used as an acronym for types of support, CARD, which corresponds to Closeness, Admonishment, Reciprocity and Durability, can be utilised as a memory tool for qualities of social support. Again using a model of flexibility, balance and buoyancy within the mentor–mentee relationship, this is graphically illustrated in Figure 1.2. Thus drinking tea and playing cards, which can depict a social support image, are easy ways to remember the main types and qualities of social support.

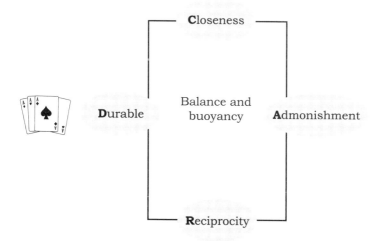

Figure 1.2 CARD – balance and buoyancy for quality of social support

Finally, it is important to note that although all qualities are needed by youth, some may have more value for a young person at particular times. For example, when a young person is dealing with a bereavement, issues of closeness to a mentor may come to the fore. Conversely in times of needing help to care for a sick parent over a long period, durability from the mentor (the capacity the mentor offers to depend on him or her) may be more important for the young person.

Sometimes social support can be harmful for young people

It is vital to remember that whereas utilising social networks to help youth in need is an effective intervention, it has definite limitations. Professionals may overlook the negative effects of a mentoring intervention on youth and those who are close to them. Over time the burden of care-giving can be extreme and mentors who provide support can despite their best intentions become 'burned out' both physically and emotionally. Furthermore, a mentor's capacity to offer social support may wax and wane depending on what is going on for that person at any point in time. For example, a mentor who is befriending a young person may suddenly find it very difficult to continue to offer support as a result of her husband becoming very ill or her losing her job. It is important to remember that life events for mentors can impair their capacity to help. Additionally, in certain contexts social support though well intended may in fact be harmful for the recipient. An anxious mentor who regularly over-protects a mentee may disable the young person in terms of readiness to deal with issues for him- or herself. In such a case the over-production of emotional and advice support may be to the detriment of the mentee.

Finally, sometimes the cost for the mentee in receiving help may exceed any benefits from the support provided. In certain situations it may not be worthwhile to receive help because of difficulties in the relationship with the mentor. For example, a teen mother who is receiving parenting advice from her mentor may initially find the support helpful but this could then change. If the mentor becomes increasingly critical of the parenting style of the mentee, becoming so negative that tension and animosity become the norm, the help, though valuable, is outweighed by the stress it induces for the youth. In this thankfully rare case, the discontinuation of help from the mentor would be preferable for the young person. This emphasises why rigorous supervision of matches is required.

Box 1.3: Key learning points

1. Having good quality of support available that involves close relationships is important to youth.

2. It is important for mentees to reciprocate support with mentors.

3. Young people can benefit from sensitively provided constructive criticism.

4. Mentors can act as dependable durable supporters to mentees.

5. Sometimes not all support from others is helpful.

Social support needs throughout adolescence

Just as maturation from childhood to adulthood is a journey rather than a destination in life, so also the social support needs and potential purposes of the mentoring relationship change and differ for young people. While this developmental journey for a young person can last for a long period and go from as young as 12 to 20 years of age, here we divide the process into early and late adolescence and consider both in terms of social support and mentorship needed.

Early adolescence

For our purposes here we are describing early adolescence as starting at 12 years of age and ending at circa 16 years. The needs of young people centre on the tumultuous nature of physical, intellectual and emotional growth and change, and the move from familial to friendship and peer relationships. Typically, the need for emotional support sought in either a hidden or an overt fashion is strong and centres on coming to terms with everything from first romantic interests to achievement and adjustment in secondary education, as well as striving for successful recognition at school, hobby or civic action success. For youth in need of help from a mentor, the focus of the friendship may stay on keeping emotional support strong and providing reassurance in terms of their skills, worth, coping capacity and future potential. It should be noted that there is a view, though not a hard and fast rule, that noticeable gender differences are most common during early adolescence in terms of types of support needed and functions of youth mentoring. This implies that boys in early adolescence have a stronger need for 'doing things' than girls and hence need primarily practical support from mentors – engaging in plentiful activities, for example sport and/or music. Conversely, during early teens adolescent girls like 'talking about' issues more so than boys and hence require more emotional support from their mentoring relationships. However, it is obvious that such gender classification is not necessarily true or helpful in that many girls are equally if not more active than boys in terms of hobby and leisure pursuits and many boys need to talk out issues and require emotional support and opportunities with mentors to do so.

Late adolescence

Generally, from the age of 16 years on, during later adolescence the priorities for a young person may include preparation for moving away from home, college or career decisions, examination stress and all associated anxieties. The need for advice support is often strong for the young person as well as reassurance and sometimes knowledge of future financial support in education or training contexts. The obvious role of the mentor is to provide primarily sound advice for the mentee with respect for his or her own capacity and right to decide on future plans. Importantly in this context the mentor can act as strong back-up and reinforcement to parents, who are of course the key supporters to their adolescent offspring. Finally, in certain contexts the mentor may be able to connect an older youth mentee with employment or education possibilities. Thus, during older adolescence, the primary role of the mentor is to provide a discreet 'support cocktail' of tangible emotional and (often primarily) advice help to the mentee.

Convoying help, hidden support and social support banking

Although much of what we know regarding youth and social support was initially established in the 1970s, more recently Levitt (2005) has developed a newer concept in what she describes as a 'Convoy Model' of social network support. Rather than seeing successful and supportive relationships between youth and others as 'win or lose or all or nothing', sometimes simply utilising the good contacts of another person can be beneficial.

So, a young person appropriately engaging with his or her mentor's network and, in a way, utilising the mentor's credit and credentials can lead to support for that young person who otherwise could be left isolated. An example of this would be where a young person gains part-time weekend employment and access to income from his or her mentor's sister who runs a local corner shop. Although this gives a new meaning to the term 'it's not what you know but who you know', if such support is not abused and respectfully accessed, then it is not harmful and all parties benefit. This can be visualised as the set of the mentor relationships acting like a convoy of trucks, where one picks up the task of offering support to youth further down the line from the direct mentor contact. This gives it the name 'convoyed support'. So it is not a young person's own network which provides the ultimate support but the strong and positive network membership of another. However, accessing such indirect support is sensitive and if utilised in a disrespectful way the result could be calamitous for all concerned and even endanger the continuation of the mentor–mentee relationship. In the main, however, where a young person uses respect and good social skills, new doors of support may well be opened.

A similar emerging model for accessing support by configuring relationships, entitled 'social support banking', recommends the young people in need develop new relationships by providing acts of support to others less known to them. By formally helping others the youth can call on them in times of need to return the favour. This builds up a sense of having a body of help available if and when needed. Through a mentoring relationship a young person can be encouraged to support friends in school, perhaps in some aspect of their schoolwork, on the basis that they will reciprocate later when the youth donor needs them. It is argued that one of the strong benefits of such a model is that it gives the young person the reassurance of having a known supply of support to turn to if needed, which in itself is hugely important, whether or not it is ever utilised. Finally, Bolger and Amarel (2007) have highlighted the importance of hidden support or support that is provided more discreetly, suggesting that where a young person does not realise he or she is being helped, the benefits that accrue are greater. This implies the need for social support banking to be enabled in a discreet 'below the radar' fashion and for donors and recipients not to make too big 'a deal' of the arrangement. Here the role of the mentor may be key to ensure that direct support and support from other networks or support banks created for the mentee are all provided discreetly. In the earlier example regarding the mentee who got a part-time job in the shop, he did not know that his mentor had set up the work invitation for him. He was under the impression that he was doing a favour for the mentor's sister by responding to her offer of work. So in this case the help from the mentor remained hidden.

Box 1.4: Key learning points

1. The support needs of youth differ at various times throughout adolescence.

2. Hidden and convoyed support are useful methods for offering support.

3. Support banking is one way of contriving support for youth in need and where utilised, mentors can act as gateways to help.

Conclusion

In this chapter we have explored the meaning of social support including definition, sources, types and qualities. In particular the role of social support for youth as mentees has been outlined. The challenges and caveats to a supportive relationship that benefits the young mentee while being a positive experience for mentors have been outlined. The importance of caring relationships, perceived support and matching need to provision of help from mentors have been emphasised. In the next chapter we will move from conceptualising social support and youth mentoring (meaning of social support) to uncover how best to assess the social support available to youth and the role of assessing ways that mentors can enhance support provision for mentees (measuring social support).

References

Bolger, N. and Amarel, D. (2007) 'Effects of social support visibility on adjustment to stress: Experimental evidence.' *Journal of Personality and Social Psychology 92*, 3, 458–475.

Cutrona, C.E. (1996) *Social Support in Couples: Marriage as a Resource in Times of Stress.* London: Sage Publications.

Cutrona, C.E. (2000) 'Social Support Principles for Strengthening Families: Messages form America.' In J. Canavan, P. Dolan and J. Pinkerton (eds) *Family Support: Direction from Diversity.* London: Jessica Kingsley Publishers.

Dolan, P. (2010) 'Youth Civic Engagement and Support: Promoting Wellbeing with the Assistance of a Unesco Agenda.' In C. McAuley and W. Rose (eds) *Child Well-Being: Towards a Better Understanding of Children's Lives.* London: Jessica Kingsley Publishers.

DuBois, D.L., Holloway, B.E., Valentine, J.C. and Cooper, H. (2002) 'Effectiveness of mentoring programs for youth: A meta-analytic review.' *American Journal of Community Psychology 30*, 2, 157–197.

Levitt, M.J. (2005) 'Social relations in childhood and adolescence: The convoy model perspective.' *Human Development 48*, 28–47.

Putnam, R.D. (2000) *Bowling Alone: The Collapse and Revival of American Community*. New York: Simon & Schuster.

Thompson, R.A. (1995) *Preventing Child Maltreatment Through Social Support: A Critical Analysis*. Thousand Oaks, CA: Sage Publications.

Tracy, E. and Whittaker, J. (1990) 'The social network map: Assessing social support in clinical practice.' *Families in Society: The Journal of Contemporary Human Services 71*, 8, 461–470.

Veiel, H. and Baumann, U. (eds) (1992) *The Meaning and Measurement of Social Support*. New York: Hemisphere.

Weiss, R. (1974) 'The Provision of Social Relations.' In Z. Rubin (ed.) *Doing onto Others*. Englewood Cliffs, NJ: Prentice Hall.

Chapter 2

Assessing Social Support for Youth within a Mentoring Context

Introduction

This chapter focuses on how best to measure the sources, types and amounts of social support for young people generally and for mentees more particularly. Based on this assessment process, a method for planning the enlistment of more and better support is outlined, which can be used in the context of a youth mentoring relationship. Purposely, this chapter is very descriptive in its nature as the aim here is to give the reader a 'practical grasp' on how best to go about enabling a young person to assess his or her support network and understand how it is (or is not) working for him or her. In the course of doing so, we also consider limitations of the assessment processes and relevance of poor or toxic social network membership. Importantly, throughout the chapter there is an assumption that young people self-assess their network (as best practice) as it enables a more accurate and empowering method. So the role of youth workers and others including mentoring case managers is to act as enablers rather than as directors.

One of the criticisms of the mentoring movement is that it can be sometimes assumed that a young person in need almost automatically requires a mentor when in fact this may or may not be the case.

Sometimes, hidden to professionals and others, there is a natural bank of support which may suffice for the young person (Pinkerton and Dolan 2007). Additionally, this untapped support might be available on a long-term basis if conditions allow the relationships involved to flourish. So at the outset, there are three key considerations in the social support assessment process of young people experiencing adversity that apply within a mentoring context. First, from the assessment prior to the decision to assign a mentor, does the young person have someone who can play a similar supportive role already available in his or her network? Second, if a mentor is required how best can the mentor support the young person? Third, how can a social support assessment ensure that long-term natural supporters are kept active during the mentoring relationship and mobilised at the match? In short, from the use of a social support assessment the following four key questions in the utilisation of mentoring can be answered:

1. Is a youth mentor needed to provide support to the young person?

2. If so, what types and amounts of help might be accessed through that friendship?

3. During the match are the young person's other sources of support including family and friends continuously engaged?

4. At the end of the match is there a plan to make sure the young person has existing or additional natural support available?

We now commence with a four-step description of the process of support assessment and interventions utilising the four 'A's. These are:

1. **A**pproaching the subject of social support with young people – how to do it, what it means and why we all need support.

2. **A**ssessing available help – to get a picture of who a young person has on offer to provide help and how he or she relates with network members.

3. **A**nalysing this social support landscape to judge how the network is working, including the types and amounts of support available.

4. **A**ccommodating and planning for new or enhanced support sources by developing a support plan and contract.

From this, two key social support assessment tools are described. First, the Social Network Questionnaire (SNQ) is outlined in order to assess who is in the young person's network and what is the quality of the relationships therein. Second, once who is available and how they are valued by the respondent have been established, the Social Provision Scale (SPS) is described as a tool to establish how the 'network works' for the young person regarding they types and amounts of help on offer. Finally, a sample social support contract for future support enlistment is provided.

Using the 4 'A's

The assessment process for gauging and planning for more support should take place over four sessions – usually of 45 minutes' to one hour's duration and ideally at a location where the young person is most comfortable, possibly his or her home. In addition, some aspect of a 'treat' for him or her should be included towards the end of each session – for example going for a game of pool or a coffee. The work should be completed by a worker known to and trusted by the young person and the process assumes the relationship is well established. The process is sensitive and confidential, involving one-to-one working, so good practice and common sense should apply. The format is briefly described here as occurring over four one-hour weekly sessions:

Session 1: **A**pproaching the subject of social support with young people – how to do it, what it means and why we all need support

In this session the topic of needing support is introduced and discussed with the young person and includes discussion of the simple fact that all of us need support to survive and thrive. Once agreement is reached on this basic principle, the option of assessing the youth's access to help is introduced and outlined by the worker. This includes the prospect of self-assessment of support by the young person and the process over the coming further three sessions culminating in a new social support plan for him or her. Importantly, at the end of the session, whether the young person agrees or not to go ahead with a social support assessment, it is key that he or she is reassured of their right to know and decide on what is best.

Session 2: **A**ssessing available help – to get a picture of who a young person has on offer to provide help and how he or she relates with network members

The following week at the commencement of Session 2 the young person should be provided with a 'check-in' by the assessor to ensure that he or she is still happy to proceed (in some cases a young person will have changed his or her mind in the intervening days). Assuming agreement, the process of completing the two assessment tools, the SNQ and the SPS, ensues (see later in this chapter for administration descriptions). A simple check-in by the assessor on how the young person experienced completing the self-reporting tools is useful to gauge whether the youth is in any way upset or bothered. Finally, before the session 'treat', it is useful to remind the young person that next week's session will focus on his/her analysing the results of the assessment.

Session 3: **A**nalysing this social support landscape to judge how the network is working, including the types and amounts of support available

In Session 3 the young person completing the assessment should again be given reassurance (see advice for commencement of Session 2 above). The focus of this session is to complete an assessment of the results from both the SNQ and the SPS. The assessor may ask questions of the young person in relation to whom he or she chose to be in the network and how much support may be derived from any individual nominee, but it is solely up to the young person to decide if it is useful support or if there is enough help available from individual nominees.

Session 4: Accommodating and planning for new or enhanced support sources by developing a support plan and contract

In this, the final of the 'A' sessions, the focus is twofold. First, the objective is to complete a 'reprise of highlights' on what is important and positive about the young person's network of support – that is, who helps and how much (solely as perceived by him or her). The second and key function of Session 4 is to enable the person to plan ahead in order to enlist more support from existing supporters or to work on introducing new sources of help. It may also include the young person deselecting people from the network, for example friends who are destructive and very personally critical of him or her. A sample network plan is outlined later in this chapter. Finally, it is crucial that the young person receives affirmation for having completed the four sessions and is offered the opportunity to give feedback on the assessment process including ways it could have been constructed better on the part of the assessor (if possible). Often youth will declare that they discovered that they had a lot more support available than they thought, and some will seek to complete a follow-up assessment in six months' time to see if their support plan is working. They may or may not seek the support of their mentor in this process.

Guide to administering the social support assessment tools with young people

Tool 1: Finding out who is in the young person's network – using the Social Network Questionnaire (Cutrona and Russell 1987, amended by Dolan 2003)

The SNQ, developed by Cutrona and Russell in 1987 and further amended by Dolan (2003), is a short itemised question sheet, which accesses information regarding an individual's perceptions of sources of support and of the overall quality of a young person's individual social network relationships. Whereas the SPS (shown later) provides information on the level and types of support on offer from network members across key areas of social support, the SNQ assesses who is in the network, the relationship of the nominee to the central network member and an overall satisfaction rating per person is identified.

The SNQ is a straightforward tool which can be easily administered in the context of establishing a baseline for sources of support and quality of relationships. It is a one-page questionnaire with a back-up information/question sheet. Completing the SNQ involves three distinct steps. First, respondents are asked to list on the form who is in their social network, including family members and friends as well as relevant others, to a maximum of 14 nominations. If the young person identifies more than 14 nominees he or she is asked to rank order these into the top 14 choices. Second, having identified who is in their network, respondents are then asked to fill in three columns in respect of each nominee. In the first column they must specify whether or not each nominee lives in their household. They are then asked to indicate in the next column the relationship between the respondent and each nominee with a distinction between close friends and other friendships. Finally, in the third column each respondent is asked to rate the overall quality of his or her relationship with each nominee across three limited choice responses. These responses include those with whom the relationship is currently bad; those with whom it is pretty much half good and half bad; and those with whom the relationship is good. Having answered this question, the respondent has completed the SNQ. The questionnaire takes on average about 15 minutes to complete.

Scoring the SNQ

Each completed SNQ is easily scored. In the first instance, in terms of sources of support, each young person completes the SNQ and is scored separately by the number of nominations with sub-groups for sources – for example, siblings, friends, extended family. In addition, where a member is identified as living at home with the respondent, this nominee is given a numerical value. Finally, regarding quality of relationships, where a youth rates their relationship with a member as bad, this is given a value of '0'. Where he or she deems the relationship as half-and-half this is given a value of '1', and where the relationship with the network member is good this is valued at a score of '2'. Thus, in terms of rating social networks, it is possible to score the perceived quality of relationships within any one respondent's network by use of a quantitative score per respondent and per network nominee. In sum, a young person can identify the number of network supporters, the number of network members living in his or her home, and the type and quality of relationship between the respondent and various nominees. This quantitative aspect of the tool has two benefits. First, repeated administrations allow for cross-tabulation between the changing perceptions of young people in respect of the nature of their social networks at different times. Second, the 'score' and rating have strong meaning for youth, who can compare across relationships and over time rather than just talk about how they get on with or feel about others. Forkan (2010) found that the aspect of scoring both of the tools described here (the SNQ and SPS) was deemed to be a key value for youth.

Whereas the SNQ gives a comprehensive assessment of respondents chosen and of the perceived set of network supporters, like any other social support assessment tool, such as the Social Network Map (Tracy and Whittaker 1990), it does not compensate for recent history issues. For example, a young person who would normally select a particular trusted close friend in their network, but is interviewed on the day after a major altercation with that friend, may out of anger omit this key person from his or her network listing. Conversely, a person could be included purely on the basis of a one-off recent supportive intervention which occurred just prior to the interview. In a true sense, in these examples, the exclusion of one person and the inclusion of another are out of context and the picture given of the network is essentially false. In order to try to compensate for this potential limitation, the authors recommend using the SNQ as a repeated measure over time. The SNQ is shown in Figure 2.1.

Tool 2: Finding out how the network is 'working' – using the Social Provisions Scale (Cutrona and Russell 1987, amended by Dolan 2003)

Once it is established from the SNQ who is in the young person's network and how they are rated, we recommend using the SPS, which measures perceived availability of social support by type and quantity of support. The SPS can be summarily described as 'quantitative' in that it enables an overall score to be established for a young person in respect of perceived social support. It measures support across types, amounts and sources of support. The SPS can be used repeatedly over time with the same young person leading to a measure for patterns of social support. Unlike most other social support assessment tools, the SPS is unique in that it can quantify social support by a scoring mechanism which also accesses qualitative data on the specific nature of support available across Weiss's well recognised types of support (Weiss 1974). Thus, each SPS question matches one of our TEA (see Chapter 1) four types of support catagories as shown in Table 2.1.

Table 2.1 Matching 'TEA' to the Social Provision Scale

Types of support (TEA)	Corresponding SPS question
Tangible (T)	Are there friends you can depend on to help you, if you really need it?
Emotional (E)	Do your relationships with your friends provide you with a sense of acceptance and happiness?
Esteem (E)	Do you feel your talents and abilities are recognised by your friends?
Advice (A)	Is there a friend you could trust to turn to for advice, if you were having problems?

Thus, the SPS establishes the extent to which ample support is perceived to be available by the young person across specific areas – for example, advice support, tangible support, esteem and emotional support. The version demonstrated in Figure 2.2 was developed by Dolan (2003), in collaboration with the original authors of the tool, Russell and Cutrona, into this adolescent friendly version.

The SPS measures forms of support from four sources: friends, parents/carers, siblings and other adults (including, where appropriate, mentors). In addition, in order to support the young person's understanding and comprehension of the questions and the form itself, a series of repeated 'four picture prompt' symbols are used. Occasionally and in some cases the use of these prompts might help a young person with a literacy or comprehension problem in the task of completing the SPS. For example, in asking the young

ID REF. No: DATE :

SOCIAL NETWORK QUESTIONNAIRE
(Cutrona and Russell 1987, amended by Dolan 2003)

INSTRUCTIONS: Please list below under 'NAME'

- First, the people you see and spend time with during a typical week. You only need to write first names of initials of all the people you see and talk to during a normal week. This would include the people you live with.

- Second, any other people whom you consider your close friends (not already listed). A close friend is a person with whom you really communicate and in whom you can confide about feelings and personal problems. The friendship is valued because of the warmth, caring, and emotional sharing it provides. *You may want to include your mentor, but you do not have to do so: it is your choice.*

- Third, the people whom you consider your casual friends (not already listed). These are people with whom you mainly do activities such as shopping, school work, sports activities, etc.

- Fourth, any relative to whom you feel close (not already listed).

- Finally, if there are other important people in your life who have not already been noted, please write them under 'NAME' also.

The following questions should be answered for each person you've just listed. Score your response next to each name. The column letters refer to the questions below.

A. Does 'NAME' live in your home?
   ✓ = YES
   ✗ = NO

B. What is 'NAME's relationship to you?
   01 = MOTHER
   02 = FATHER

03 = CARER/STEP-PARENT/FOSTER PARENT

04 = BROTHER/SISTER

05 = OTHER RELATIVE

06 = CLOSE FRIEND

07 = OTHER FRIEND

08 = OTHERS IN RESIDENTIAL SETTING (NOT LISTED AS
       FRIENDS)

09 = PROFESSIONAL PERSON (PLEASE LIST TYPE)

10 = OTHER PERSON, PLEASE STATE

C. Is most of your contact with 'NAME' positive (make you feel good), or negative (make you feel bad)?

1 = BAD

2 = HALF AND HALF

3 = GOOD

NAME	A	B	C

Figure 2.1 The Social Network Questionnaire

person to respond to question number 4, the interviewer would state to the interviewee: 'I am asking you the question written above the picture of the girl on the phone.' The interviewer would then ask the question regarding advice support and the respondent would then choose 'No', 'Sometimes' or 'Yes' in response. Thus, young people complete the SPS by giving each source grouping a rating against each question which relates to a form of support, via a limited choice. The interviewee completes the form by going through each source grouping rather than by type of support on offer, starting with friends, and then continuing with parent(s)/carers, siblings and other adults including mentors (should one already be engaged), in this order. The 16-item questionnaire takes on average no more than 10 minutes to complete. Needless to say, however, some young people will want to discuss why they gave particular nominees a positive or negative rating and thus the qualitative aspect of the tool kicks in and of course should be discussed by the adult completing the assessment.

Scoring the SPS

Each completed SPS is scored separately with an overall total score per youth. In order to establish this total score, each question is scored individually by simply allocating each of the three possible responses a value as follows:

No = 1

Sometimes = 2

Yes = 3

All completed questions are scored and totalled for an overall score. In respect of scoring across sources, all groupings are given the same value. This means that, on the basis that there are four sources containing four questions each, the range of possible total scores go from a minimum 16 (i.e. where in all cases the response is 'No') to a maximum possible score of 48 (where in all cases the response is 'Yes'). However, in cases where a respondent does not have any siblings, this naturally would reduce the minimum and maximum potential scores. Figure 2.2 displays an outline of the SPS tool.

In answering the next four questions, please think about your current relationships with your *friends*. If you feel a question accurately describes your relationships with your friends, you would say 'yes'. If the question does not describe your relationships, you would say 'no'. If you cannot decide whether the question describes your relationships with your friends, you may say 'sometimes'.

1. Are there friends you can depend on to help you, if you really need it?

    NO   SOMETIMES   YES

2. Do your relationships with your friends provide you with a sense of acceptance and happiness?

    NO   SOMETIMES   YES

3. Do you feel your talents and abilities are recognised by your friends?

    NO   SOMETIMES   YES

4. Is there a friend you could trust to turn to for advice, if you were having problems?

    NO   SOMETIMES   YES

In answering the next set of questions, please think about your current relationships with your *parent(s)/carer.*

5. Can you depend on your parent(s)/carer to help you, if you really need it?

    NO   SOMETIMES   YES

6. Do your relationships with your parent(s)/carer provide you with a sense of acceptance and happiness?

    NO   SOMETIMES   YES

7. Do you feel your talents and abilities are recognised by your parent(s)/carer?

    NO   SOMETIMES   YES

8. Could you turn to your parent(s)/carer for advice, if you were having problems?

    NO   SOMETIMES   YES

In answering the next set of questions, please think about your current relationships with your *brother(s) and/or sister(s)*.

9. Can you depend on your brother(s)/sister(s) to help you, if you really need it?

    NO   SOMETIMES   YES

10. Do your relationships with your brother(s)/sister(s) provide you with a sense of acceptance and happiness?

    NO   SOMETIMES   YES

11. Do you feel your talents and abilities are recognised by your brother(s)/sister(s)?

    NO   SOMETIMES   YES

12. Could you turn to your brother(s)/sister(s) for advice, if you were having problems?

    NO   SOMETIMES   YES

In answering the next set of questions, please think about your current relationships with *any other adult person in your community* — for example, a teacher, sports coach or other adult who you know and who supports you.

13. Can you depend on other adult(s) you know to help you, if you really need it?

    NO   SOMETIMES   YES

14. Do your relationships with this adult(s) provide you with a sense of acceptance and happiness?

    NO   SOMETIMES   YES

15. Do you feel your talents and abilities are recognised by this adult?

    NO   SOMETIMES   YES

16. Could you turn to another adult for advice, if you were having problems?

    NO   SOMETIMES   YES

Figure 2.2 The Social Provisions Scale

Summary of key measurement functions of the Social Provisions Scale

Sources of support: The top score for each source (parents, friends, siblings and other adults) is 12, while the minimum is 4. A total score can be arrived at when all the scores from the four sections (maximum = 48; minimum = 16) are added together. This score indicates where the young person accesses support and/or where he or she has little or no perceived support.

Types of support: Scores can also be calculated for the four types of perceived support (concrete, emotional, esteem and advice). This is very useful since it reveals what types of support the respondents perceive they are getting and where the gaps are – information that can be valuable in planning an intervention. It should be noted that a balance of support is required across the four types of perceived support to achieve optimal functioning.

Table 2.2 Summary of scoring for the Social Provisions Scale (sources and types of perceived support)

Friends	Maximum	12	Minimum	4
Parents/carers	Maximum	12	Minimum	4
Siblings	Maximum	12	Minimum	4
Other adults	Maximum	12	Minimum	4
Total:	**Maximum 48**		**Minimum 16**	
Types of support				
Concrete	Maximum	12	Minimum	4
Emotional	Maximum	12	Minimum	4
Esteem	Maximum	12	Minimum	4
Advice	Maximum	12	Minimum	4
Total:	**Maximum 48**		**Minimum 16**	

Research on using the SNQ/SPS in the context of an Irish youth mentoring programme by Alan Quinn (a Master's graduate at the National University of Ireland, Galway, who is also a field manager on the Foróige Big Brothers Big Sisters of Ireland programme) has highlighted two important issues. First, while many assessments of the social support landscape of potential mentees utilise the views of referrers and parents they often overlook the view of the young person, which is a very obvious oversight. Quinn's research (2011) highlights the need to have the mentee act as central investigator into his or her own support network as a matter of right and pragmatically to get a 'true picture'. Second, he highlights the temptation for caseworkers, parents or mentors to assume both that the young person understands the tool fully and that they as adults can assess its meaning better than the mentee. His research using critical reflective practice highlights caution regarding both these fronts and recommends allowing the mentee to take the lead regardless of the views or enthusiasm of other adults.

Don'ts and do's in assessing social support in youth mentoring

Tracy and Whittaker, in their pioneering work on social support measurement (1990), have summarised key pointers including things to do or not do in assessing social support. We have amended these to fit the specific context of youth mentoring as shown in Box 2.1.

Box 2.1: Don'ts and do's for social support assessment in youth mentoring

Don't assume a young person needs a mentor to begin with – **Do** look to see if there are natural positive supporters available who are willing to help.

Don't automatically assume that having plentiful support from a large pool of supporters is better – **Do** recall that there is no perfect size of social network. Sometimes young people get on better with a smaller resource of willing helpers.

Don't assume that 'what you see is what you get'. The perceived levels and amounts of help that a person identifies may on closer examination not be accurate. Discussion to clarify this is required – **Do** listen to what a young person perceives in relation to his or her support network.

Don't think that changes in the network of a mentee will automatically bring more support and **Do** remember that sometimes changes in social behaviour by the young person may also be required.

Don't focus solely on the young person accessing more support from others and **Do** encourage him or her to donate help.

Don't overlook the exchange of help in the network between other members, for example how friends can club together to support the mentee and **Do** look out for good 'TEA' or the presence of all types of tangible, emotional, esteem and advice support as well the presence of CARD support (Closeness, Admonishment, Reciprocity and Durability).

Don't encourage the young person to expect instant positive change and **Do** remember that gaining better support has to be actively worked at and takes time.

Don't assume that as mentor you can solve all the problems your mentee is experiencing and **Do** remember that sometimes care-giving can be stressful – so care for the carer.

Source: Adapted from Tracy and Whittaker (1990)

Developing a support-building contract with a young person post-assessment

For young people to assess their social support network as being perfect and needing no adjustment is very rare; generally they will seek improvement. However, being specific about how to work with a young person on enlisting better support can be tricky and sensitive. On occasions it may be that completing the assessment leaves the young person feeling very dejected at the lack of support or toxic nature of certain relationships. If, for example, he or she has a mental health problem, the issue of entering into the assessment in the first place needs careful consideration. However, thankfully, most children, youth or adults who successfully self-assess their support demonstrate a capacity and interest in improving their supply of personal support. A simple way of building on the learning of the assessment is first to assess the key results of the SNQ/SPS and to complete this task with the young person. The guide sheet in Box 2.2, developed by Tracy and Whittaker (1990) and again amended by the authors here for the specific purpose of youth mentoring, can be helpful.

Based on the key messages from this sheet the central worker can (with inclusion of parent(s)) develop a 'cooperative contract' with the young person as conductor, to enlist social support which may or may not include a youth mentoring programme. This then acts as a guiding chart for the young person to ensure that their social support landscape improves over time. Figure 2.3 provides a template for such a contract.

Box 2.2: Social support
Ten key assessment guidelines

1. Who is in the young person's network?

2. What does the young person see as strengths and capabilities of the network?

3. What are the gaps in his or her social support needs?

4. Which network members are identified as responsive, effective, accessible and dependable?

5. Is reciprocity an issue?

6. Which network members are critical of the young person and can or should these members be deselected from the network?

7. What obstacles or barriers exist to accessing better support?

8. How are social support needs prioritised in relation to other issues the young person faces, presenting problems or needs?

9. Would mentoring help this young person gain more support and, if so, how can a mentor help address some of the issues from the list 1 to 8 above?

10. What does the mentee think would be his or her top three priorities to access more or better social support?

Source: Amended from Tracy and Whittaker (1990)

The strengths of my network are:

_____

_____

_____

What I want to change (my goal):

_____

_____

_____

Barriers I need to consider:

_____

_____

_____

Steps to reach my goal:

1. _____

2. _____

3. _____

4. _____

(If relevant) specific ways my mentor can help me to reach my goal:

5. _____

6. _____

7. _____

8. _____

_____   _____

Signature (young person)   Signature (caseworker)

Figure 2.3 Cooperative contract for getting more support (adapted from Tracy and Whittaker 1990)

One simple way to use the contract is for the young person to assess whether all forms of 'TEA' are present and if so, in satisfactory amounts. Where specific types of support are deemed by a person to be lacking, establishing the reasons, steps to enhance needed support and any possible barriers may prove useful. This method, which should be kept simple and purposeful, is further illustrated in the accompanying Social Support Action Plan shown in Table 2.3.

Table 2.3 Social Support Action Plan

Types of support from X person	Available in the last month Satisfactory ✓ Unsatisfactory ✗	Reason	Steps to access more or less help or to remove person from network	Risk/ barriers
Tangible				
Emotional				
Esteem				
Advice				

Finally, after at least one social support assessment has been completed and the results distilled into key messages which are then built up to a youth-led work plan in the form of a contract, repeating the SNQ and SPS will help. This enables the young person to establish whether there has been improvement, no change or deterioration in the support he or she can muster over time. Very often adolescence is tumultuous and particularly so for youth in need; by taking this longer-term 'bigger picture', a young person will not be overinfluenced by the occurrence of any one negative life event and be able to weigh up positive as well as negative interactions with others.

At a broader level, completing the contract will help the young person select or deselect others from his or her network. A possible role for a mentor if engaged is to act almost as a 'silent supporter' to the young person during his or her process of reflection, but at the same time to be there to advise if requested to do so.

Conclusion

This chapter has described in detail how to conduct a social support assessment and how (if appropriate) this can be used in a youth mentoring context. It could be argued that while we all use different sources in our networks for differing purposes, identifying at least one reliable alliance may be the key objective. This person (or people) is typically someone with whom a young person has an important relationship who can be turned to for help under any circumstances. The purpose of the assessment process is to use the SNQ and SPS or some of the many other available social support tools as 'personal youth charts' to help young people decide what works best for them and, where appropriate, if having a mentor is a good and possible option.

References

Cutrona, C.E. and Russell, D. (1987) 'The Provisions of Social Relationships and Adaptation to Stress.' In W.H. Jones and D. Perlman (eds) *Advances in Personal Relationships* (volume 1). Greenwich, CT: JAI Press.

Dolan, P. (2003) 'Adolescents in adversity and their networks of social support.' School of Social Work and Social Policy, Queen's University Belfast (unpublished doctoral thesis).

Forkan, C. (2010) 'Building evidence on how to support adolescents through a comparative tracking of their perceived social support outcomes.' UNESCO Child and Family Research Centre, National University of Ireland, Galway (unpublished doctoral thesis).

Pinkerton J. and Dolan, P. (2007) 'Family support, social capital, resilience and adolescent coping.' *Child and Family Social Work 12*, 219–228.

Quinn, A. (2011) 'Examining how to involve a mentor in improving an adolescent's social supports for life post-mentoring.' UNESCO Child and Family Research Centre, National University of Ireland, Galway (unpublished master's thesis).

Tracy, E.M. and Whittaker, J.K. (1990) 'The social network map: Assessing social support in clinical practice.' *Families in Society: The Journal of Contemporary Human Services 71*, 8, 461–470.

Weiss, R. (1974) 'The Provision of Social Relations.' In Z. Rubin (ed.) *Doing onto Others*. Englewood Cliffs, NJ: Prentice Hall.

Chapter 3

Good Practice in Mentoring Programmes

Introduction

As we saw in the Introduction, evaluations of youth mentoring programmes show that involvement in relationships with unrelated adults can result in benefits for young people. But the research indicates that not every mentoring programme will produce these results and that good relationships supported by adequate infrastructure are needed in order to achieve success (Sipe 2002). The body of research into mentoring has identified a range of factors that are associated with good outcomes from mentoring practice. This chapter is designed to provide an overview of the types of practices associated with effective mentoring programmes. It is not designed to be a definitive account of how to run a mentoring programme. Those wishing to establish a programme should refer to the resources at the end of the book and contact relevant organisations for advice and guidance.

This chapter looks first at issues related to programme design and the core practices that underpin reputable mentoring programmes. It then moves on to highlight characteristics of the mentors, mentees and the mentoring relationship that are associated with better outcomes. The chapter also looks at the challenges and dilemmas faced in mentoring practice and offers some suggestions for how these can be addressed.

Programme design

All mentoring programmes should have a clear vision and set out the principles and ethos according to which they are managed. They should include the following:

- The overall goals and expectations for the programme in terms of outcomes for young people, volunteers and the wider community.

- How the programme will be governed and the roles of management and staff.

- A profile of the target young people for the programme (for example in terms of age, ethnic background and needs) and how their participation in the programme will be secured (i.e. where referrals will come from).

- The characteristics of the volunteers who will be recruited as mentors. For example, some programmes specifically look for college students or senior citizens whereas others are open to suitable volunteers of all ages and backgrounds.

- The type of mentoring that will be offered and the purpose it will serve (i.e. the purpose could be broadly about positive support for young people or there may be specific objectives regarding career or behavioural issues).

- The expectations regarding frequency of contact, duration of matches, where matches will meet, etc.

- The practices that will underpin the programme (see below).

- Procedures for quality assurance, monitoring and evaluation.

- Policies and procedures in relation to child protection, staff development, financial management, volunteer support, dealing with complaints and other matters deemed to be of importance to the organisation.

It is important that the aspirations regarding what mentoring relationships are expected to achieve are not too ambitious. As highlighted in the Introduction, the research suggests that where mentoring is targeted at modest outcomes, such as improved aspirations on the part of young people, and values their own identities and resources, it can be successful in making gains on its own terms. However, it is less successful when targeted at a particular goal (such as entry into employment or reducing offending behaviour). The approach adopted throughout this book is that youth mentoring relationships should be designed to enhance the support available to young people, bearing in mind the complexities associated with the provision of support (addressed in Chapter 1).

Box 3.1: A vision for a youth mentoring programme

The Foróige BBBS of Ireland programme manual clearly sets out the mission for the programme as encapsulated in the following definition and explanation:

> To make a positive difference in the lives of young people through a professionally supported one-to-one relationship with a caring adult volunteer. The volunteers, as Big Brothers or Big Sisters, are friends, mentors and positive role models who assist these young people in achieving their unique potential.

The programme is based on the idea that a created relationship between an older and younger person will act to prevent future difficulties or be a support to young people facing adversity in their lives. A caring adult friend can help to build positive assets for young people, enabling them to have a commitment to learning and a positive sense of self and the future. The presence of this non-familial caring adult is expected to make a difference in the social and emotional development of the young person. Rather than focusing on 'deficits' or what the young person lacks, the programme adopts a positive youth development approach that addresses the young person's full range of needs and the competencies required to help them to become a productive and healthy adult.

Source: BBBS of Ireland (2010)

Core policies and procedures

Mentoring programmes generally undertake the following procedures as core elements of good practice:

Volunteer screening

The screening of volunteers is one of the most important practices associated with mentoring programmes. It must be undertaken to ensure that the mentors selected are suited to the role, are in a position to commit to meet weekly for at least one year and have been vetted/checked to ensure that it is safe to match them with a young person. Police vetting and checking of two or more references, a home visit and an in-depth interview form part of the mentor assessment in many programmes. As well as investigating the suitability of adult volunteers to act as mentors for young people, this process provides an opportunity to explore their interests and personalities which will help in making the match. It is also important that the mentor has realistic expectations regarding their potential impact and is aware of the challenges associated with the role.

Young person's assessment

The assessment process for young people should ensure that they are interested (want a mentor) and suitable for the programme, and that their parent or guardian is supportive of their involvement. Some of the tools described in Chapter 2 can be used to assess the young person's support network and gain a greater understanding of whether the intervention would suit.

Volunteer training

Before they are matched, it is important that mentors receive training to prepare them for the role of mentor. This training can highlight the problems and difficulties that often arise in mentoring relationships, reassuring future mentors that they will not be alone in dealing with particular issues. Research has shown that mentor training is important in terms of building the mentor's sense of efficacy in relation to the match and helping the mentor to sustain their commitment if the going gets tough.

Making the match

Making a good match is of critical importance as the mentoring relationship is more likely to be enjoyable for both parties and to 'go the distance' if the mentor and young person have common interests. Matching procedures should, therefore, take into account the preferences of the young person, their parents and the mentor. Mentoring programme staff place a lot of emphasis on getting the right match for the young person. This may mean that a suitable match is not 'on the books' and the young person may be asked to wait for some time until a suitable mentor is found. This is preferable to making a match that is unlikely to be a success.

At the matching stage, it is also important that all the people with a 'stake' in the match are clear regarding what is expected of them. It is useful to ask young people, parents, mentors and caseworkers to sign contracts setting out what is expected from them over the course of their involvement with the programme. It is also important that the privacy and integrity of the young person is protected in the matching process. While the programme staff will know a lot about the young person (and about any family issues or difficulties) as a result of the assessment process, it is important that only basic 'need to know' information is shared with the mentor (such as age, where the young person lives and his or her interests). This ensures that mentors accept the mentees on their own terms and do not enter the relationship with preconceived ideas about their life. It is then up to the young person to share as much or as little information as he or she sees fit.

Match supervision

Supervision of matches is an important component of the programme. Through supervision, the caseworker can help with any problems that arise and ensure that the match is proceeding safely. Problems that often arise in the first few months include difficulty in communication (for example the young person won't answer the phone), the young person being very quiet or not turning up for meetings. The caseworker can work with both parties to identify the reasons for the problems and come up with solutions. The requirements for supervision in reputable mentoring programmes include initial contact with the parent, young person and volunteer within two weeks of the match, monthly telephone contact with the volunteer, parent and/or young person during the first year and quarterly contact with all parties for the duration of the match.

Match closure

Mentors are generally asked to commit for a minimum of one year. Matches can end for a variety of reasons – for example, the young person and his or her family may move away, the mentor's personal circumstances may change, either party may become ill or decide that they simply do not want to continue. It is good practice to include clear processes for match closure, including a final evaluation of the match. Programme staff generally try to ensure that the match closure is undertaken in a way that minimises any disappointment to the young person and is fully respectful of him or her. The closing process should include a celebration of the achievements in the relationship and set out clearly the expectations for further contact (if any) between the mentor and mentee. The match closure should also pay attention to the needs of the young person and how he or she can access support on an ongoing basis.

Record-keeping

Accurate and up-to-date records of key events relating to all matches should be kept on file in order to provide the agency with a systematic record of case activity, which facilitates continuity of service delivery, supports case management and provides transparency in terms of the match supervision. It is valuable to include a system of auditing of files whereby an external person checks the files of every caseworker to ensure that they are up to date and in line with expectations.

Programme manual

It is good practice to have a comprehensive programme manual that clearly sets out the policies and procedures governing all aspects of the programme. While the core elements of the programme are unlikely to change, the manual should be subject to continuous review and updating. The standards and procedures should clearly set out how the following will be undertaken:

- screening of volunteers
- assessment of young people
- matching
- supervision
- match closure.

It is vitally important that there is consistency and integrity in the application of these procedures. Failure to observe these practices is likely to increase the risks to young people, parents, mentors and programme staff involved in the programme. It is good practice to establish an auditing system to check that there is fidelity to the programme manual at all times.

Celebration and recognition of the contribution of programme participants

Many mentoring programmes hold formal events to recognise the achievements and contributions of mentors and mentees. Such events are valuable in terms of boosting morale and enabling people to see that they are part of a bigger community that is dedicated to the same ends. Such events may provide a psychological boost to matches and help to ensure that matches last for as long as possible (MENTOR/ National Mentoring Partnership 2005).

Collaboration with relevant agencies and groups

As highlighted in the Introduction, youth mentoring is not a panacea and should not be considered a stand-alone solution to a young person's needs. Mentoring programmes can be enhanced by having strong links with other agencies working with young people, which can act as a source of referrals for the programme and can also be sources of support for young people and their mentor. For example, the BBBS of Ireland youth mentoring programme was developed as an add-on service for young people taking part in the youth service provided by the host organisation, Foróige. Foróige saw the need for one-to-one work for some young people attending their services and felt that mentoring was a valuable volunteer-led model to address this need. Research into the programme showed that the young people and their families knew and trusted Foróige and thus were more likely to agree to take part in the mentoring programme. The mentoring programme also benefited from the referral networks and support structures in place between Foróige and other organisations, such as social services and schools. Because they knew the young people attending the youth service, the youth workers employed through Foróige had a good understating of which young people would benefit from a mentor and could continue to work with them while they were taking part in BBBS. The newly developed BBBS programme also benefited from being able to allow matches to meet on the premises of youth clubs and cafés, which overcame the issue of mentors and mentees not having places to get together. Foróige staff believe that integrating the mentoring programme into the larger youth organisation enabled the emergence of a more holistic approach to meeting the young person's needs and provided synergies and benefits that would not have accrued had mentoring been developed as a stand-alone programme (Brady 2010).

Role of programme caseworkers

The people who oversee the general running and management of mentoring programmes on a day-to-day basis are generally known as 'caseworkers'. Their duties include taking referrals and assessing the suitability of young people for the programme, recruiting and training volunteers, making and supervising matches, providing training and support to caseworkers in partner organisations, co-ordinating advertising and information meetings for volunteers and organising group activities for participants. They generally have relevant qualifications (in a youth or social care field) and are experienced in working with young people. Programme caseworkers are generally expected to complete a range of training courses relating to all aspects of the programme.

Characteristics and approach of the mentor

There is a considerable body of research regarding the attributes, traits and approaches that mentors need in order to form a successful relationship with a young person. Research suggests that the most

successful mentors are those who have prior experience in l
roles or organisations, are sensitive to the issues in young people s
lives, have a strong sense of personal efficacy in relation to their ability
to be a good mentor and a good degree of self-awareness regarding
their own strengths and weaknesses (Dunphy *et al.* 2008).

A body of research evidence also draws our attention to the fact that
some styles of mentoring may be more effective than others. DuBois
and Neville (1997) believe that greater understanding of relationship
characteristics and their implications for mentoring effectiveness could
aid in the development of more successful programmes. For example,
when Slicker and Palmer (1993) evaluated the impact of a school-
based mentoring programme on 86 at-risk students, the initial results
showed no difference between the intervention and control groups.
However, when the differences between those students who were
effectively mentored versus those who were ineffectively mentored
were evaluated, they found that effectively mentored students had a
lower dropout rate.

Morrow and Styles (1995) identified two broad categories of
relationship, which they labelled as 'developmental' and 'prescriptive'.
Developmental mentors devote themselves to developing a strong
connection to the youth, centering their involvement on developing
a reliable, trusting relationship. They place a strong emphasis on
maintaining the relationship and ensuring it is enjoyable. Only when
the relationship is strongly established do they start to address other
goals, such as strengthening the youth's capacity to deal with stress.
They include the mentee in the decision-making process about
activities and are willing to change their plans according to the youth's
preferences. Morrow and Styles' (1995) research into mentoring
relationships in the BBBS programme in the USA found that youth in
developmental relationships reported feeling a considerable sense of
support from their adult friend – believing he or she would be there
for them in times of need. 'Just listening' and 'being able to talk about
anything' were perceived by youth as helpful in helping to resolve or
cope with difficulties. Providing opportunities for fun was one of the
'mainstays of the relationship'. These volunteers were more likely to
make the relationship last long enough to be helpful to the youth.

On the other hand, *prescriptive* relationships are those in which the
goals of the volunteer are primary, with the adult setting the pace and

ground rules for the relationship. Morrow and Styles (1995) found that the mentors in these relationships believed that their efforts could 'transform' the young person within a year or two. In this way, according to Morrow and Styles (1995), prescriptive mentors set the basic ground rules of the relationships beyond the capacity of most early adolescents. Both the mentor and the youth are frustrated in these relationships. These mentors do partake in some fun activities but were more likely to push for 'good for you' activities and offer fun as a reward for 'good behaviour' (1995, p.v).

Morrow and Styles (1995) also found that the majority of matches in which mentors took a developmental approach met on a regular and consistent basis and only a small proportion ended early. By contrast, matches in which the mentors took a prescriptive approach only met sporadically and the majority had ended early. The following quote from Russell Beal from the Buddy Programme in New Zealand reflects the broad consensus in the literature that mentors who see their role as contributing to a young person's social or emotional well-being will be more successful than those who are more controlling (Dunphy *et al.* 2008, p.25):

> the word contribute is used to convey the sense that youth mentoring needs to take a strengths based approach to the children. They are not problems to be fixed or even students to be taught, they are young people with innate capacities and personal strengths to be encouraged. More in the sense of 'a garden to be grown' than a computer to be fixed.

Characteristics of the young person

Young people from a variety of backgrounds can potentially benefit from youth mentoring and mentoring programmes can be designed to take into account the interests, needs and aspirations of various target groups. Some mentoring programmes are targeted at specific groups of young people, such as those disengaged or at risk of disengaging from the education system or those in contact with the youth justice or probation services. Other programmes are targeted at young people with more general needs, such as being socially isolated, being shy or withdrawn or having early signs of anti-social behaviour, or because it is felt that, due to their personal or family circumstances, they woul benefit from the one-to-one support of a mentor.

The young person is expected to be an active participant in the mentoring relationship. As we saw in Chapter 1, reciprocity is an important aspect of supportive relationships and a characteristic of successful relationships is that the mentor enjoys it as much as the young person. In assessing the suitability of young people for a mentoring programme, therefore, it is important that they have the capacity to form a relationship with a mentor and that their needs are not so great that they are unsuitable for matching with a volunteer. For example, very challenging behaviour on the part of the young person may be too much and too difficult for a voluntary mentor to deal with.

Jean Rhodes (2005) also draws attention to the fact that young people who have been damaged by relationships in their lives may find it harder to form an attachment with their mentor. As a result, it may take longer for them to build up trust and to benefit from the relationship if they do at all. On the other hand, young people who have had positive relationships in their lives may be more ready to 'hit the ground running' and quickly build up trust and derive benefits from the relationship. This unfortunately means in some cases that 'the rich get richer' (i.e. that those with better supports in their lives gain more from the mentoring relationship) than those who need it more. However, the gains for young people who develop relationships in spite of previous failed relationships can be stronger.

As discussed in Chapter 1, mentoring relationships can be valuable in enhancing the support available to young people where, due to family structure or circumstances, the parent or parents are simply not in a position to provide as much support to the young person as they would wish. Research into the BBBS mentoring programme in Ireland found that the outcomes from mentoring were particularly strong for young people not living with both parents compared to young people living with both of their parents. After 18 months, the disparity in outcomes between young people from one-parent families and those from two- had lessened considerably, which suggests that mentoring may be able to supplement the support available to young people in one-parent families (Dolan *et al.* 2011).

Characteristics of the mentoring relationship

The most valuable relationships for young people are those that are characterised by more frequent contact and emotional closeness and last for six months or longer. The frequency of contact between mentors and youth greatly influences the extent to which processes of change have an opportunity to occur. Greater amounts of time spent together are associated with higher levels of support in mentoring relationships and increased likelihood of the young person nominating the mentor as a significant adult in his or her life.

According to Sipe (2002), one of the strongest conclusions that can be drawn from the research on mentoring is the importance of providing mentors with support in their efforts to build trust and develop a positive relationship with youth. Programmes need to develop an infrastructure that fosters the development of effective relationships, namely screening, orientation and training and support and supervision. In other words, one of the best ways to support mentees is to support their mentors. Likewise, Grossman (quoted in Louw 2002) found that, to prevent matches from ending prematurely, a consistent support structure needs to be in place offering ongoing support and supervision of the match.

Parra *et al.* (2002) found that mentors' self-efficacy beliefs were important in terms of how the mentoring relationship developed, and suggest that initial programme training should be strong enough to instil sufficient levels of skill and confidence in mentors. Ongoing availability of staff support is necessary to sustain high levels of mentor efficacy, while opportunities for mentors and youth to participate in agency-sponsored activities were also beneficial in helping bonds to develop. Parra *et al.* (2002) make the point that mutual support groups are a low cost way of providing support and encouragement to mentors. Yet, DuBois *et al.* (2002) note that initial training or orientation to mentors was provided to mentors (71% of studies reviewed), but that efforts to provide ongoing training once relationships have begun are much less common (23% of studies reviewed). They note that factors such as increased cost and reluctance to make excessive demands on volunteer mentors hinder the development of such infrastructure.

Research indicates that providing opportunities for matches to meet with other matches on a regular basis can be beneficial (Brady 1 Dolan 2005; Cavell *et al.* 2009). It is also valuable to facilitate volunteer mentors to meet as a group without their mentees so that they can share experiences, offer mutual support and so on. Programmes should allocate a budget to allow this to happen and regularly.

Common challenges faced in mentoring programmes

Many mentoring programmes struggle to find sufficient male volunteers which means that it can be difficult to meet the strong demand for mentors for young males. There is a need for programmes to be creative in addressing this issue. One of the factors that inhibits men from volunteering is the fear that allegations of abuse may be made against them (Brady 2010). Many people with an aptitude for working with young people have taken part in child protection training which advises them not to be alone with a young person. Thus, the appeals of mentoring programmes for them to take part in a one-to-one relationship appear counter-intuitive. Programmes facing these issues have found that it can be useful to target predominantly male organisations such as rugby and football clubs and appeal to their members to take part. Potential volunteers who may not have considered volunteering for the reasons just outlined may be reassured when they hear about the rigorous safety practices underpinning mentoring programmes. It may also lead to a snowball effect, whereby one person volunteers and their friends and teammates then come forward when they hear how positive the experience has been. Another initiative to address the volunteer shortage involved the BBBS of Ireland programme running an annual combined media campaign through local print media and radio stations to 'recruit 30 male mentors in 30 days'.

In rural areas in particular, it can be difficult for matches to find places to go. It is good practice for the mentoring programme to arrange a place, such as a community centre, youth café or youth club which is available to matches on a drop-in basis once a week or more frequently if required. The match can use the premises to play board games, use computers, cook, play table tennis or do other activities depending on the facilities available. In summary, by providing spaces and opportunities to meet, matches are more likely to be close and durable.

Monitoring and evaluation

The importance of good monitoring and evaluation procedures are widely accepted in youth services. Such procedures can help to find out if the service is meeting the needs of the young people it is working with and realising the aims, vision and values of the organisation. Furthermore, monitoring and evaluation data can also help to demonstrate to current and potential funders and other stakeholders that the programme is robust and is meeting its objectives. In an era of scarce resources, it can be a case of 'survival of the fittest', with organisations who are able to provide evidence that what they do is effective being more likely to receive funding.

The evaluation of mentoring is fraught with difficulty. At policy level, there can be pressure to show that mentoring has an impact on 'hard' measurable outcomes such as school grades, employment and crime rates in order to justify its funding investment. On the other hand, research shows that mentoring is most effective when targeted at softer outcomes and that there is less evidence of progress in relation to the 'harder' outcomes (Pawson 2006). Critics argue that, for young people with multiple challenges in their lives, what is considered 'success' will vary from person to person depending on their starting point and that top-down indicators are unable to capture this. Dunphy *et al.* (2008) argue that mentoring can enhance the protective factors in young people's lives, which in turn can help them to deal with adversity in life and achieve positive outcomes. They argue that it is these protective or nurturing factors that should be measured, as an increase in these dimensions are likely to predict positive outcomes for young people.

Therefore, it is useful to establish a strategy or framework for evaluation of the programme to ensure that the organisation has the relevant data to enable it to make decisions regarding service improvement. This includes agreeing desired outcomes and indicators and putting in place procedures to establish whether the outcomes are being achieved.

Two key types of data can be collected for monitoring and evaluation purposes: programme data and outcomes date. Both are now described.

Programme data

Operational or performance data related to the programme is valuable to provide feedback regarding whether the programme is operating in a manner that is safe, effective and cost efficient (Dunphy *et al.* 2008, p.39). Some of the indicators of such performance include:

- *Coverage*: How many matches were made through the programme? How many volunteers applied and how many were accepted? Did the programme reach its target group? What linkages were made with other organisations, including inward and outward referrals?

- *Strength and intensity*: Did the implementation include as much of the 'dose' as intended? What percentage of matches lasted for 12 months or more and what percentage ended early?

- *Quality*: Were services provided at an acceptable level of quality? For example, were staff trained to the appropriate level? Were child protection guidelines followed at all times? Were the core programmes and practices adhered to at all times? What is the ratio of caseworker to matches – in other words, how many matches are managed by each caseworker?

- *Perceptions*: How was the programme experienced by participants? Did they feel it was worthwhile and of a good standard? Did they think it made a difference to them? How did they think it could be improved?

- *Costs*: What is the cost of each mentoring relationship?

From an operational perspective, these indicators provide feedback regarding critical areas of programme performance. For example, if the percentage of matches that end early is high, there is a need to look at the reasons why this is the case. If the most common reason is that volunteers are withdrawing from the programme for personal reasons, it may indicate a need for a more rigorous assessment of volunteers to ensure that only those who are likely to make a year-long commitment are selected. It may also indicate that more training and support is needed for volunteers. As the programme develops from year to year, it is valuable to plot these indicators in a graph to see if any trends are evident. For example, if the ratio of caseworkers to matches increases and there is an increase in the number of matches that end early, it may indicate that the quality of support available to mentors is not sufficient. It is important to review these issues with programme staff and to talk to all stakeholders to find out the reasons for these trends. Given the importance of ensuring that matches are supported to meet as frequently as possible and to last as long as possible, this type of data is critical in terms of highlighting issues that may be impacting on the outcomes from the programme.

Outcomes data

Outcomes refer to changes in behaviour, values, skills or relationships that have occurred as a result of the mentoring programme. The outcomes that are measured should be those that the programme was designed to impact on. For example, if the programme objectives relate to educational objectives, such as staying in school or having a positive attitude to school, these are the outcomes that should be measured. If the emphasis is on the development of a supportive relationship, with a view to improving the social and emotional well-being of the young person, measures related to these dimensions should be chosen.

A key challenge in assessing outcomes is proving causality – in other words, demonstrating that it was the mentoring programme and not other influences that caused the change in outcomes for the young person. Because young people are subject to many influences in their lives – through family, peers, school, community, the media – it is hard to pinpoint whether the programme has made a difference or whether another influence was responsible. Some evaluations use a control group to compare the outcomes for young people with a mentor to those without a mentor. Such experimental designs are costly and difficult, and involve an ethical issue regarding denying the opportunity to participate to the control group. However, many experimental studies of mentoring have been undertaken and have shown small but significant effects (Dolan *et al.* 2011; DuBois *et al.* 2002).

It is not feasible for small-scale programmes to undertake experimental design to assess outcomes, so what can be done? There are a number of options:

- Because the quality of the mentoring relationship is of critical importance, it is useful to ask the young people and mentors to complete a questionnaire designed to assess the quality of the relationship. The measure could be taken as part of regular quarterly reviews. This measure should provide an indication regarding the quality of the match.

- As highlighted in Chapter 2, measurement tools have been designed specifically to assess the supportiveness of mentoring relationships.

- Assessment tools can be selected to capture whether the desired outcomes have been achieved. As highlighted earlier, these outcome measures could relate to education and/or to social and emotional well-being. It is important to ensure that a baseline measure is taken at the start of the match so that the pattern of change can be assessed over time. While this will not provide causal evidence that the mentoring programme has produced these effects, it does provide useful indicative data that can show whether or not change is occurring in the way the programme intended.

Conclusion

There is a considerable body of evidence regarding the practices that are required in order for mentoring programmes to be run in a way that is safe and effective. This chapter has provided a brief overview of good practice in the areas of programme design, core practices, styles of mentoring relationship, mentor and mentee background and evaluation.

References

BBBS (Big Brothers Big Sisters) of Ireland (2010) *Service Delivery Manual and Pack.* Galway: Foróige/BBBS.

Brady, B. (2010) 'An assessment of the value and viability of youth mentoring as a policy option in an Irish context.' National University of Ireland, Galway (unpublished PhD thesis).

Brady, B. and Dolan, P. (2005) *Big Brothers Big Sisters of Ireland: Evaluation Study.* Galway: Child and Family Research Centre.

Cavell, T.A., DuBois, D., Karcher, M., Keller, T. and Rhodes, J. (2009) *Strengthening Mentoring Opportunities for At-Risk Youth.* Policy brief. Portland, OR: National Mentoring Center. Available at www.educationnorthwest.org/webfm_send/237, accessed on 18 July 2011.

Dolan, P., Brady, B., O'Regan, C., Canavan, J., Russell, D. and Forkan, C. (2011) *Big Brothers Big Sisters of Ireland: Evaluation Study: Report One: Randomised Controlled Trial and Implementation Report.* Galway: Child and Family Research Centre.

DuBois, D.L. and Neville, H.A. (1997) 'Youth mentoring: Investigation of relationship characteristics and perceived benefits.' *Journal of Community Psychology 25*, 3, 227–234.

DuBois, D.L., Holloway, B.E., Valentine, J.C. and Cooper, H. (2002) 'Effectiveness of mentoring programs for youth: A meta-analytic review.' *American Journal of Community Psychology 30*, 2, 157–197.

Dunphy, A., Gavin, B., Solomon, F., Stewart, C., Collins, E. and Grant, A. (2008) *Guide to Effective Practice in Youth Mentoring New Zealand.* Wellington: Youth Mentoring Network.

Louw, J. (2002) *The Difference an Hour can Make: An Early Outcome Study of Big Brothers Big Sisters of South Africa.* Cape Town: Research and Evaluations Services.

MENTOR/National Mentoring Partnership (2005) *How to Build a Successful Mentoring Program using the Elements of Effective Practice: A Step by Step Toolkit for Program Managers.* Alexandria, VA: MENTOR/National Mentoring Partnership.

Morrow, K.V. and Styles, M.B. (1995) *Building Relationships with Youth in Program Settings.* Philadelphia, PA: Public/Private Ventures.

Parra, G.B., DuBois, D.L., Neville, H.A., Pugh-Lilly, A.O. and Povinelli, N. (2002) 'Mentoring relationships for youth: Investigation of a process-oriented model.' *Journal of Community Psychology 30*, 4, 367–388.

Pawson, R. (2006) *Evidence-based Policy: A Realist Perspective.* London: Sage Publications.

Rhodes, J.E. (2005) 'A Model of Youth Mentoring.' In D.L. DuBois and M.J. Karcher (eds) *Handbook of Youth Mentoring.* Thousand Oaks, CA: Sage Publications.

Sipe, C.L. (2002) 'Mentoring programs for adolescents: A research summary.' *Journal of Adolescent Health 31*, 6, 251–260.

Slicker, E.K. and Palmer, D.J. (1993) 'Mentoring at-risk high school students: Evaluation of a school-based program.' *School Counsellor 40*, 327–334.

Further reading

Dunphy, A., Gavin, B., Solomon, F., Stewart, C., Collins, E. and Grant, A. (2008) *Guide to Effective Practice in Youth Mentoring New Zealand.* Wellington: Youth Mentoring Network.

MENTOR/National Mentoring Partnership (2005) *How to Build a Successful Mentoring Program using the Elements of Effective Practice: A Step by Step Toolkit for Program Managers.* Alexandria, VA: MENTOR/National Mentoring Partnership.

State of Victoria (2006) *A Guide to Effective Practice for Mentoring Young People.* Melbourne: Department for Victorian Communities, Office for Youth.

Chapter 4

School-based Mentoring

Introduction

It is widely accepted that the transition from primary to secondary school represents a key challenge for young people (Eccles 1999; Dryfoos 1990). Most will make this transition without any significant problem, but for some young people experiencing personal or family difficulties, the transition can be particularly stressful. They must cope with existing personal issues while also establishing themselves in a new and alien school environment. It is at this juncture that some young people can fall behind their peers and become alienated from school. This disconnectedness can lead to academic and peer problems, problem behaviour and eventually to leaving school early. Research has clearly shown that dislike of and alienation from school contributes to the decision to leave school early (Byrne and Smyth 2010). There are clear associations between early school-leaving and socio-economic disadvantage later in life, while participation in school is considered to be a developmental asset on the basis that young people remaining in the school system are less likely to be exposed to risk factors than those who have left without qualifications (Leffert *et al.* 1998).

Research also shows that low satisfaction with school is thought to contribute to health-compromising behaviours such as smoking and alcohol use (Samdal *et al.* 2000). Policy makers are, therefore, increasingly seeing the need for interventions designed to support young people to feel connected to and comfortable in the school environment if they are to stay in school and to succeed academically.

School-based mentoring programmes have been developed with the explicit purpose of supporting young people to connect with and do well in school.

In this chapter, the nature of school-based mentoring programmes is explored in greater detail. There are two broad types of school-based mentoring programmes. 'Cross-age peer mentoring' refers to the provision of mentoring supports to a young person by an older student within the school, while 'school-based mentoring' is the term used to describe programmes which bring adults from the community into the school to mentor students within the school setting. Table 4.1 highlights how each of these forms of mentoring is different from each other and different from the community-based model of mentoring. The key difference is that cross-age peer mentoring is undertaken by older peers, while school-based mentoring is undertaken by adults. Cross-age peer mentoring programmes are usually aimed at supporting younger students in their first year of secondary school, while school-based mentoring programmes involve mentees of all age groups within the school community. Community-based matches are generally more free in the sense that mentors and mentees can meet where they wish and engage in a wide range of activities of their choosing. Thus, there is greater potential to build a stronger relationship than in the more constrained setting of a school-based mentoring programme.

What is cross-age peer mentoring?

> Peer mentoring involves an interpersonal relationship between two youth of different ages that reflects a greater degree of hierarchical power imbalance than is typical in a friendship and in which the goal is for the older youth to promote one or more aspects of the younger youth's development. (Karcher 2005, p.267)

According to Karcher (2007), cross-age peer mentoring typically takes place in school settings as a means of supporting younger students within the school environment. Meetings between mentors and mentees normally take place weekly in a classroom, after school or during lunch and last about one hour. These meetings take place for the duration of the school year. The meetings often occur within

Table 4.1 Key differences between community- and school-based peer mentoring

	Community-based mentoring	School-based mentoring	Cross-age peer mentoring
Mentors	Mentors are adults from the community.	Mentors are adults from the community.	Mentors are older peers/students from the same school.
Mentees	Mentees are generally young people aged 10–18 years from the community.	Mentees are generally young people of all ages from the school community.	Mentees are generally young people in their first year of secondary school.
Setting	The mentor and mentee meet wherever they wish.	The mentor and mentee meet on the school grounds, usually in a room where other matches are also meeting.	The mentor and mentee meet on the school grounds, usually in a room where other matches are also meeting.
Timing	The match generally meets for one or two hours or longer every week, at a time of their choice.	The match generally meets at a prescribed time (e.g. lunchtime) every week for a set period.	The match generally meets at a prescribed time (e.g. lunchtime) every week for a set period.
Duration	Matches are expected to last for 12 months or more.	Matches are expected to last for the academic year (often just October to April).	Matches are expected to last for the academic year (often just October to April).
Focus	Can engage in a wide variety of activities, depending on their interests.	Activities are constrained by the school setting. May have an academic focus.	Activities are constrained by the school setting. Usually does not have an academic focus.
Outcomes	More likely to result in outcomes related to peer and parental relationships, emotional well-being.	More likely to result in academic outcomes, particularly where there is an academic focus.	More likely to result in outcomes related to school connectedness or peer support.

a large group, with perhaps 10 to 20 pairs engaged in individual or group-based activities (Karcher 2997, p.3). This approach is defined by the following characteristics:

- The approach to relationship building is developmental rather than prescriptive, meaning that the focus is on helping mentees to develop their character and sense of self, rather than imposing goals on the relationship. The aim is that the mentor and mentee will develop a friendship that will be of benefit, with any prescribed goals, be they academic or personal, coming second (Karcher 2007, p.5).

- The programmes typically last throughout the school year or longer, meeting 20–40 times per year. Karcher suggests that they should meet for a minimum of ten times to be considered a mentoring relationship.

- There is an age difference of at least two years separating the mentor and mentee.

- The intervention is generally not reparative, remedial or problem focused (Karcher 2007, p.6). It is not aimed at promoting academic skills, resolving interpersonal problems or addressing personal problems. While these issues may arise in conversation, they are 'by-products' and not the primary purpose of the intervention.

There is some research evidence that cross-age peer mentoring has resulted in positive effects for mentors and mentees (Karcher 2007, p.6). Studies have shown improvements in attitudes to and connectedness to school and peers, self-efficacy, grades or academic achievement, social skills and reduction of behaviour problems. Miller (2002) argues that mentees are often more amenable to receiving support from an older peer, while cross-age peer mentors develop skills and experiences that will be useful them in their later careers. Indeed he speculates that the benefits to mentors may outweigh the benefits to mentees. Powell (1997) found similar evidence of openness on behalf of mentees to working with older peers and notes that younger peers look forward to becoming mentors themselves as they get older. King *et al.* (2002) also report the benefits to both mentors and youth that can accrue from such programmes. Powell (1997) believes that peer

Box 4.1: Advantages and disadvantages of cross-age peer mentoring

Advantages

- The older student has knowledge and experience that are directly relevant to the younger student.
- It can help younger students to settle into a new school.
- It can break down barriers and form relationships between older and younger students.
- It can make the school a friendlier place as a value is placed on supportive relationships.
- It may help prevent instances of bullying.
- It helps to build leadership and helping skills in older students.
- It increases the range of possible supporters and confidantes for younger students.
- It is not costly as it is provided within the school setting.

Disadvantages

- The 'dosage' or amount of hours that mentors and mentees meet is lower than in community-based matches because the match just lasts for the school year.
- The relationships developed may not be very close due to the fact that the scope for activities and sharing experiences is limited.
- As with all mentoring relationships, there is a risk that relationships will end early or the mentor attends infrequently which may result in feelings of disappointment for the mentee.

mentoring services can help to reduce the stigma of asking for help and show both parties how to effectively ask for and provide support. She concludes that:

> Peer assistance appears to be instrumental in helping disadvantaged youth improve academically and develop feelings of belonging in school. Properly matched tutors

and tutees can develop positive personal bonds. Cross age tutoring in particular seems to foster bonds so that participants come to regard one another as surrogate siblings or extended family members. (Powell 1997, p.9)

Pawson (2004) undertook a review of research evidence in relation to the various types of mentoring programmes. He found that peer mentoring programmes don't seem to be as successful as adult/youth mentoring relationships. In particular, where mentees need to develop understanding or learning skills, support may be better provided by adults. The one exception to this involves situations where older peers are speaking from experience of a situation that they have lived through and can pass on this knowledge to younger peers. In this case of cross-age peer mentoring, the older peers are supporting younger mentees though the transition to school, a change they themselves already experienced. Pawson (2004) also recommends that goals in successful peer mentoring programmes need to be set by both the mentor and mentee themselves and that it is important to take an individual approach as peers will vary in terms of their support needs and attitudes to working with older peers. Pawson also notes that peer programmes need to be sensitive to power relations and cliques within schools, as more effective supports are provided by older peers from the majority group within the school rather than those from minority cliques.

Case example 4.1: Cross-age peer mentoring programme in Mount Pleasant Comprehensive School

Mount Pleasant Comprehensive School decided to introduce a mentoring programme for first-year students to ease their transition into the school. The principal approached a local youth organisation which had developed a model and found it great to have their support in running the programme in the school.

The programme is completely voluntary – interested first years can apply and older students can volunteer to act as mentors. All applicants are interviewed and a match is made based on mutual interests. The students all meet in the school library at lunchtime one day a week. The school nominated a teacher to act as a link co-ordinator for the programme. The link teacher facilitates the matches to meet every week and organises activities for them to do, such as quizzes and board games.

The principal has been delighted with the difference the programme has made in the school. She believes that the first-year students feel more secure at school as they have an older friend to look out for them and tell them how things are done. The older students have responded well to the responsibility they have been given and see the importance of caring for the younger students – they describe it as 'cool'. She believes that this sense of caring has reverberated beyond the programme itself and that senior students are more aware of looking out for younger students in other settings such as the canteen and on the school bus. She indicates that younger students may be more likely to talk to their mentor if something is bothering them than to approach a teacher formally. They have had incidences of issues being brought to their attention by senior students that they would not otherwise have been aware of.

The programme very much complements the school's policy in relation to pastoral care as it again emphasises the importance of making students feel welcome, secure and supported in the school environment. Parents of incoming students are very positive about the fact that mentoring is available in the school. The programme has been running in the school for five years now so first years who were mentored are now acting as mentors themselves.

The main challenge the school has faced has been the time it takes to interview all applicants and make the matches at the start of the school year. This can take a few weeks with the result that the first years may be in school for three or four weeks before they are matched. Ideally they would have their mentor in place when they start. They have also had an issue with some senior students not turning up. They have nominated a few 'floating' mentors who can be matched with a mentee in these situations.

Programme practices

Karcher (2007) emphasises that cross-age peer mentoring programmes must be well structured and properly managed in order to avoid any potential negative outcomes for the young people involved. He highlights that there is increasing evidence that cross-age peer mentoring programmes that are not adequately structured have the potential to do as much harm as good. On the other hand, adhering to good practice guidelines for such programmes can help to ensure that positive outcomes will accrue for both mentors and mentees. Based on a review of published research on such programmes, he identifies the characteristics of effective peer mentoring programmes as including the following:

Recruitment

In some schools, all first years are welcome to apply to take part in the programme, while in others particular young people are targeted for participation because it is believed that they would benefit. It is generally a good idea to include a mixed profile of mentees, to avoid stigmatising more needy young people and thus singling them out for participation. Research also suggests that the mentors recruited should have a strong social interest and sense of caring for others. Karcher and Lindwall (2003) found that mentors were more successful if they scored high on social interest rather than self-interest. Those with a stronger self-interest are more likely to approach the mentoring relationship as an opportunity to have fun with peers rather than with the objective of being a help to them (Karcher 2007, p.10).

Training

Research has shown that the self-efficacy of mentors, in other words their belief in their ability to do a good job as a mentor is a predictor of the quality of the mentoring relationship (Karcher et al. 2005). Initial training for mentors is critical to ensure that they have a good understanding of what it means to be a mentor and how to deal with any challenges that may arise. Follow-up training is also likely to be helpful, in terms of addressing any challenges that may have arisen as the relationship is progressing. It is also important that mentors are encouraged to adopt a developmental approach rather than seeing their role as that of tutor. It is useful to provide training to mentees regarding how best to seek out and utilise the support of the mentor.

Structure

All participants must be clear at the outset regarding what is expected in terms of commitment and attendance. The programme should provide enough structure to enable the matches to have fun and build rapport, while also allowing them some free time to talk and get to know each other. Many programmes provide an activity booklet for schools to provide ideas for fun activities for matches.

Supervision

Karcher (2007) emphasises the importance of ensuring that matches are supervised and monitored to check that mentors and mentees are turning up for meetings and that they are engaging with each other during meetings. Given that frequent attendance by mentors is critical to successful outcomes, if either party is not attending, it is important to find out why and encourage better commitment. It may be necessary to re-match a 'little' with another 'big' if a mentor is not showing up, whilst still paying due attention to the fact that the 'little' may be disappointed at the ending of the previous match. It is also important that an adult is on site at all times to supervise the matches to ensure that 'deviancy training' does not occur (Karcher 2007, p.10). This could include telling inappropriate jokes to their peers, 'slagging' and name calling, undermining the authority of teachers or encouraging risk-taking behaviours.

Formal endings

As with community-based matches, it is important to formally end the match and review the achievements. Many mentoring programmes celebrate and recognise the achievements of mentors and mentees and award certificates of participation. This typically forms part of the end of academic year celebrations.

School-based adult mentoring

As described earlier, school-based mentoring involves a relationship between a young person and an adult, with meetings taking place during school hours. Because the relationship involves a younger person and an older adult, it is similar to community-based mentoring in many ways, but there are also crucial differences. To begin with, as highlighted earlier there is less scope for flexibility regarding activities and meeting times. However, it is possible that the more timetabled approach would suit some potential mentors who appreciate knowing when they are meeting with their mentee. It is also possible that school-based mentoring can reach young people who would not have access to a mentor through a community-based programme. Solomon *et al.* (1996) argue that successful school-based mentoring programmes may increase social support within the school by bringing in caring adults from the local community, for example retirees (see the Experience Corps programme based in the USA).

Herrera *et al.* (2011) point out that the school-based nature of this programme may work in different ways to help young people. For example, school-based mentoring may be particularly effective in helping young people to develop social skills and to communicate with peers and teachers at school. If the mentoring relationship can impact on young people's relationships with teachers and peers, it is possible that they will feel more settled at school and perform better academically. They also point out that participation in school-based activities can increase young people's sense of belonging or connection at school and their liking for school (Eccles and Barber 1999). Increasing connectedness to school in turn has been found to provide positive benefits. For example, Simons-Morton *et al.* (1999) undertook an investigation into the relationship between student–school bonding and problem behaviour at school. They found that improved student–school bonding was associated with increased school adjustment and a reduction in problem behaviour at school.

Box 4.2: Advantages and disadvantages of school-based mentoring programmes

Advantages

- Young people who are having difficulties at school can receive additional one-to-one support.

- The range of supporters available to the young person is increased.

- They can make use of school resources, such as facilities and staff, and thus do not cost as much as community-based programmes.

- They bring new resources and perspectives into the schools that can help students and teachers.

- The more structured timetable and shorter time commitment may appeal to some potential mentors over the more open-ended timetable of community-based mentoring.

Disadvantages

- The relationships developed may not be very close due to the scope for activities and sharing experiences being limited and its taking place in a school, which can be perceived as a restrictive environment.

- As with all mentoring relationships, there is a risk that relationships will end early or the mentor attends infrequently which may result in feelings of disappointment for the mentee.

The growing body of research on school-based mentoring has yielded somewhat mixed results regarding its effectiveness. A consistent theme in research relating to school-based mentoring is the reduced 'dosage' of school-based programmes. In other words, mentors and mentees tend to meet for less time every week and for a shorter duration than in other mentoring programmes. Herrera *et al.* (2000) reports that on average school-based programmes are half the dosage of community-based programmes (6 hours per month vs. 12 hours per month). This has implications for the outcomes that can be expected from such interventions as it may be the case that mentees simply don't receive enough mentoring to make a significant difference to them. The meta-analysis of 55 youth mentoring programmes undertaken by DuBois *et al.* (2002) showed smaller effect sizes for school-based mentoring programmes than for community-based models. Portwood and Ayers (2005) suggest that the timetabling constraints of the academic year and the school day may minimise the scope for frequent contact, emotional closeness and longer relationships, all of which are associated with stronger outcomes from mentoring programmes.

Wheeler *et al.* (2010) report that three high profile evaluations of school-based mentoring programmes have been completed in the USA since 2008. Their meta-analysis of the findings of these three studies found evidence of favourable outcomes in six areas – reduced truancy, reported presence of a supportive non-familial adult relationship, perceived scholastic efficacy (i.e. perceptions of one's academic abilities), school-related misconduct, peer support and absenteeism. The authors conclude that one year of participation in a school-based mentoring programme tends to have modest effects on these outcomes. However, as discussed in the following paragraph, the findings of the BBBS evaluation (Herrera *et al.* 2011) raise questions regarding whether these effects are sustained after the match ends.

Herrera *et al.* (2011) undertook one of the largest studies of school-based mentoring, involving 1139 young people aged 8 to 18 years participating in the BBBS of America school-based mentoring programme. The youth were randomly assigned to either a treatment group, who received a mentor, or to a control group, who did not receive a mentor. Outcome measures related to school-related performance and attitudes, problem behaviours and social and personal well-being. Measures were collected at baseline, nine months and 15 months. They found that in the first year of involvement in the programme, participants received five months of mentoring, which is typical of school-based programmes because they tend to start a few months into the school year and finish before the end of the school year. After this short period of mentoring, the study showed that the group of young people who had been mentored had improved academic outcomes, albeit modest, and that they were more likely to report having a 'special adult' in their lives who provided them with support. When the youth were surveyed again at 15 months' post-baseline (i.e. in the autumn of the following school year), the relative improvement for mentored youth in academic performance was no longer evident, but they were still more likely to report having a special adult in their lives. No improvements were found in relation to social and personal well-being. The authors conclude that the presence of mentors in schools can help students to improve their academic performance during the school year when matched. However, this advantage appears to 'decay' when the match ends (Herrera *et al.* 2011, p.357). Herrera *et al.* believe that there is a need for further experimental research to establish whether continuing mentoring relationships into a second or third year would result in the enhanced outcomes being sustained over a longer period. BBBS of America responded to the evaluation by promoting strategies to enhance the effectiveness of their programme. These include enhanced volunteer training and support, lengthening match relationships and providing agency support throughout the summer months (Wheeler *et al.* 2010).

In summary, therefore, the research on school-based mentoring suggests that it can be effective in improving school connectedness and academic outcomes but that the improvements may not be sustained beyond involvement in the programme. Further research is required to establish whether longer mentoring relationships would result in outcomes being sustained over time.

Programme practices

The programme practices described in Chapter 3 that relate to community-based matches are largely relevant to school-based mentoring programmes. There are a number of features that are particular to the school environment that are worthy of note, however. School-based mentoring programmes are often provided by an outside agency and it is essential that there is good buy-in and cooperation between the school and the mentoring agency. Herrera (2004) found that agency support for school-based mentors is critical in creating strong, long-lasting mentoring relationships. The mentors' perceptions of the support available to them from the agency was a critical influence on their assessment of the success of their own mentoring relationship.

Conclusion

There is considerable scope for mentoring in school contexts, including mentoring by older peers (known as cross-age peer mentoring) and by adults from outside the school (known as school-based mentoring). These programmes can produce different outcomes than community-based programmes, and research indicates that outcomes tend to be more related to school connectedness and academic performance than well-being and family/peer relationships as are commonly outcomes from community-based programmes. However, because they are generally run within the constraints of the school year and the daily timetable, a key challenge in these programmes is ensuring enough 'dosage' or mentoring hours to make a difference to mentees.

References

Byrne, D. and Smyth, E. (2010) *No Way Back? The Dynamics of Early School Leaving*. Dublin: Economic and Social Research Institute.

Dryfoos, J.G. (1990) *Adolescents at Risk: Prevalence and Prevention*. New York: Oxford University Press.

DuBois, D.L., Holloway, B.E., Valentine, J.C. and Cooper, H. (2002) 'Effectiveness of mentoring programs for youth: A meta-analytic review.' *American Journal of Community Psychology 30*, 2, 157–197.

Eccles, J.S. (1999) 'The development of children ages 6 to 14.' *The Future of Children 9*, 2, 30–44.

Eccles, J. and Barber, B.L. (1999) 'Student council, volunteering, basketball, or marching band: What kind of extracurricular involvement matters?' *Journal of Adolescent Research 14*, 10–43.

Herrera, C. (2004) *School-based Mentoring: A Closer Look*. Philadelphia, PA: Public/Private Ventures.

Herrera, C., Sipe, C.L. and McClanahan, W.S. (2000) *Mentoring School-aged Children: Relationship Development in Community-based and School-based Programs*. Philadelphia, PA and Alexandria, VA: Public/Private Ventures in collaboration with MENTOR/National Mentoring Partnership.

Herrera, C., Baldwin Grossman, J., Kauh, T.J. and McMaken, J. (2011) 'Mentoring in schools: An impact study of Big Brothers Big Sisters School-Based Mentoring.' *Child Development 82*, 1, 346–361.

Karcher, M.J. (2005) 'Cross age peer mentoring.' In D.L. DuBois and M.J. Karcher (eds) *Handbook of Youth Mentoring*. Thousand Oaks, CA: Sage Publications.

Karcher, M.J. (2007) *Research in Action: Cross-Age Peer Mentoring*. Alexandria, VA: MENTOR/National Mentoring Partnership.

Karcher, M.J. and Lindwall, J. (2003) 'Social interest, connectedness, and challenging experiences: What makes high school mentors persist?' *Journal of Individual Psychology 59*, 293–315.

Karcher, M.J., Nakkula, M.J. and Harris, J. (2005) 'Developmental mentoring match characteristics, correspondence between mentor's and mentee's assessment of relationship quality.' *Journal of Primary Prevention 26*, 2, 93–110.

King, K.A., Vidourek, R.A., Davis, B. and McClellan, W. (2002) 'Increasing self esteem and school connectedness through a multidimensional mentoring program.' *Journal of School Health 72*, 7, 294–299.

Leffert, N., Benson, P., Scales, P., Sharma, A., Drake, D. and Blyth, D. (1998) 'Developmental assets: Measurement and prediction of risk behaviors among adolescents.' *Applied Developmental Science 2*, 4, 209.

Miller, A. (2002) *Mentoring Students and Young People: A Handbook of Effective Practice.* London: Routledge.

Pawson, R. (2004) *Mentoring Relationships: An Explanatory Review.* Working paper 21. London: ESRC UK Centre for Evidence-based Policy and Practice. Available at www.kcl.ac.uk/content/1/c6/03/46/19/wp21.pdf, accessed on 16 May 2011.

Portwood, S.G. and Ayers, P.M. (2005) 'Schools.' In D. DuBois and M.J. Karcher (eds) *Handbook of Youth Mentoring.* Thousand Oaks, CA: Sage Publications.

Powell, M.A. (1997) 'Peer tutoring and mentoring services for disadvantaged secondary school students.' *California Research Bureau 4*, 2, 1–10.

Samdal, O., Wold, B., Klepp, K.I. and Kannas, L. (2000) 'Students' perception of school and their smoking and alcohol use: A cross-national study.' *Addiction Research 8*, 2, 141–167.

Simons-Morton, B.G., Crump, A.D., Haynie, D.L. and Saylor, K.E. (1999) 'Student school bonding and adolescent problem behaviour.' *Health Education Research 14*, 99–107.

Solomon, D., Watson, M., Battistich, V., Schaps, E. and Delucchi, K. (1996) 'Creating classrooms that students experience as communities.' *American Journal of Community Psychology 24*, 719–748.

Wheeler, M.E., Keller, T.E. and DuBois, D.L. (2010) 'Review of three recent randomized trials of school-based mentoring.' *Social Policy Report 24*, 3, 1–24.

Chapter 5

Providing Social Support through Mentoring for Specific Groups of Young People

Introduction

There are important nuances relating to mentoring for specific populations of young people. In this chapter we explore a range of typical youth populations where they face risk or adversity and mentoring has been utilised as a method of social support. Here we consider in turn youth with a mental health problem, the context of youth justice services, youth leaving care, immigrant youth, and young people with a physical or intellectual disability. Finally, we consider the issues in relation to providing youth mentoring from an intergenerational perspective. It should be noted that it is not possible in this chapter to cover all contexts of adversity which young people endure; so, for example, youth living in abject poverty or young people who suffer familial domestic violence are not considered here. However, the core principles of youth mentoring, how it can be best provided and what is known to work supported by some case examples are outlined here. This in turn can be applied to other contexts for young people.

Mentoring youth with a mental health difficulty

Why is having a mentor helpful to a young person with a mental health issue?

In many ways, supporting a young person who experiences mental health difficulties is one of the most obvious roles for any adult or peer mentoring programme. Ideally, it encompasses all core types of support (TEA) with particular emphasis on emotional helping, and all four qualities of good network relationships (CARD), with strong attention to the mentor being non-criticising and administering plentiful esteem support. Mentors can help to alleviate their mentee's sense of distress and improve their perceived well-being. Mentors can help enable their mentee become more confident and encourage them to be active citizens and engaged in their community which in turn can enable better resilience simply by turning the young person's attention away from themselves and their problems. In itself this can be a very positive by-product of the mentoring relationship.

However, care-giving to someone with a mental health problem can be difficult and over time stressful for the donor. This is of particular relevance within the context of providing social support through mentoring for youth with mental health difficulties. The mentee may be focused solely on his or her own problems and show little insight to the needs of the mentor, unable to demonstrate basic interest in the mentor, the mentor's family or their lives. Over time the mentor may become disheartened and less inclined to stay in the relationship as a result of this. It can be hard to give support if one does not get it in return.

In what ways can mentors support youth with a mental health problem?

A key aspect of the mentoring relationship is for the mentor to remain a close, warm and stable influence on their mentee, both in times of distress and when things are going well for him or her. Importantly, the mentor should not see their mentee as someone with a problem but as a young person with much to offer in the relationship and who just needs some additional support. For some mentees the context and content of their mentoring relationship may differ, with some youth preferring to stick to participating in activities with their mentor and not really discussing their problems. Conversely, other youth may actively seek a friend whom they trust and with whom they can discuss their feelings and use as a confidante. Mentors can be particularly helpful in this regard as they are not family and are not tied up in the young person's peer friendship network, thus enabling the mentor to be a little 'outside' and allowing the mentees to feel they can talk more freely. Mentors for youth with mental health difficulties can also give hidden support by keeping a 'discreet watch' by providing low key support in relation to the mental health sustenance of their mentee.

Mentoring programmes for youth with mental health issues

It is important that those who manage the mentoring relationship provide the mentor with support so he or she can in turn continue to offer similar support to the young person. Having an alliance (i.e. a case manager) available for the mentor to check in with in case of a concern, or even just to touch base with informally, is crucial (Sipe 2002).

Issues for the mentee such as severe anxiety over what others would see as trivial, difficulties sleeping and keeping concentration can have a direct impact on the task of keeping the mentoring relationship functioning and running smoothly during regular contact (Brugha 1995). The issue of how and what the mentor knows of the mentee's mental health problem must also be handled sensitively with the young person not being left with a feeling of being a 'case' and thus beholden to the mentor. Similarly, the mentor needs to have some understanding of the features of mental ill health in adolescence; for example, the mentor should be able to cope with mood swings and occasional or frequent unreasonableness on the part of the young person. Having said this some research indicates that youth with a mental health problem regardless of gender make an ongoing effort and engage well with the mentors (more so than with family or friends) and successfully complete engagement and maintenance in the relationship (Mead *et al.* 2010). This act of participation in the relationship on the part of the young mentee itself can be a successful outcome for a community mentoring programme.

Case example 5.1: Peter (15 years)

Peter has suffered with an obsessive compulsive disorder (OCD) since the age of nine. He has attended a psychologist and participated in two behaviour control treatment programmes as well as taking medication for the disorder. He self-reports a strong degree of variability with the problem, going from times where he does not feel compelled to participate in compulsory routines to spells where he can hardly function from hour to hour without going through a series of ritualistic movements. Peter is an active youth leader in the local youth club and through this project he was matched with a mentor, Paul, an adult mentor volunteer who lives in the local area. Early on in the relationship Peter shared with Paul issues relating to his need for obsessive behaviour but purposely asked his mentor not to discuss this with him any further. This Paul agreed to without further any questioning of Peter.

Paul and Peter meet weekly and enjoy sports. Both are interested in jogging and keeping fit and they go on runs together, usually on Saturday mornings. For Peter the fact that Paul knows of his OCD and does not bother him about it, but still accepts him as a friend to have fun with, is key and in itself this is a source of strong sustenance to Peter. For example, each time they meet, for fun one of them has to come up with an unusual word, the meaning of which the other has to then find, but only from asking others and not using dictionaries or the internet. Recently Peter asked Paul what 'Hippopotomonstrosesquippedaliophobia' means. It took Peter three weeks out to discover that it means someone who has a fear of long words. This is a good example of how Paul and Peter share good fun together. Peter clearly sees Paul's role not to be a therapist but just a good friend who cares for and about him.

Key reading

Brugha, T.S. (1995) 'Social Support and Psychiatric Disorder: Recommendations for Clinical Practice and Research.' In T.S. Brugha (ed.) *Social Support and Psychiatric Disorder, Research Findings and Guidelines for Clinical Practice.* Cambridge: Cambridge University Press.

Mead, N., Lester, H. and Chew-Graham L.G. (2010) 'Effects of befriending on depressive symptoms and distress: Systematic review and meta-analysis.' *The British Journal of Psychiatry 196*, 96–101.

Sipe, C.L (2002) 'Mentoring programs for adolescents: A research summary.' *Journal of Adolescent Health 31*, 251–260.

Mentoring for youth justice/youth offending

There has been considerable interest from a policy perspective in the potential of mentoring to reduce offending behaviour among young people. These initiatives recognise that young people engaged in anti-social behaviour are often experiencing a range of socio-economic and personal challenges and believe that young people would benefit from having a stable one-to-one relationship with an adult helper. Mentoring initiatives are designed to provide practical and advice support in helping the young person to identify issues in their lives and take action to address them. For example, through their connections, mentors may link young people to opportunities in the areas of education, employment or recreational activities and help them with tasks such as preparing a CV or filling in a job application. Mentors can also provide emotional support to young people to help them to cope, as well as esteem support through recognising their talents and achievements. They can also model pro-social behaviour, making young people less likely to engage in crime. Furthermore, the time spent with the mentor might reduce the time that the mentee has to offend (Jolliffe and Farrington 2008).

Mentoring programmes in the area of youth justice generally encompass a number of features, of which mentoring is one part. For example, in the UK the Mentoring Plus initiative run by Crime Concern and Breaking Barriers consists of education, training, social and recreational activities alongside one-to-one mentoring. Similarly, mentoring projects supported by the Youth Justice Board also aim to improve young people's prospects in education and employment and to help them to overcome issues in their personal lives.

There may be a compulsory element to some mentoring programmes, whereby young people are mandated to participate by the courts. Whether participation is voluntary or mandated has implications for the nature of engagement by the young person with the programme.

There is little conclusive evidence that mentoring programmes targeted at offending young people are effective in reducing criminal behaviour. UK studies of mentoring programmes by Newburn and Shiner (2005) and St James-Roberts *et al.* (2005) did not find any evidence of a reduction in offending or criminal behaviour among mentored participants. While a review of studies by Jolliffe and Farrington (2008) found evidence that mentoring reduced offending by four to ten per cent, they urge caution in the interpretation of this finding on the basis that it was studies of a lower methodological quality that showed this result, while more rigorous studies did not find that mentoring had an impact on reoffending.

While there is no evidence to suggest that these programmes achieve their primary objective of behavioural improvements, the studies show that mentoring can result in positive outcomes in other areas. In particular, mentoring can be successful in reintegrating young people into mainstream education and training activities and can lead to improved literacy and numeracy skills. Gains were also seen in the areas of family relationships and involvement in the wider community (Philip and Spratt 2007).

As with all mentoring interventions, issues of programme implementation have significant influence on the outcomes that can be realised. Research has highlighted the following issues as particularly important:

- Dosage, or how much of the intervention is needed for positive outcomes to accrue, is critical to success. St James-Roberts *et al.* (2005) found that more gains were made where the mentoring relationship lasted at least ten months and young people were consistently engaged. Likewise, Jolliffe and Farrington's (2008) review of 48 studies in this field highlighted that programmes in which the mentor and mentee spent more time together (five hours or more per meeting) and met at least weekly were more successful in reducing re-offending.

- Again, reflecting the main body of mentoring research, the openness of the participants to engaging with their mentor and the degree of trust built up between them is critical to success. Mentoring programmes targeted at youth offending often have high dropout rates, possibly due to the fact that young people may be required to participate and leave when they have fulfilled the minimum requirements. Programmes can experience a high turnover of mentors and staff, which is likely to be due to the fact that the behaviour of mentees can be challenging. This highlights the need for careful mentor and staff recruitment, retention and ongoing training and support.

- As highlighted above, mentoring interventions in this area are often provided in the context of other programmes or initiatives. Evidence suggests that mentoring is most effective when combined with education, training and drawing up contracts of acceptable behaviour rather than delivered on a stand-alone basis (Jolliffe and Farrington 2008). Realistic goals should be set, underpinned by an achievable pathway setting out how change will occur.

Studies in the areas of mentoring and youth justice again highlight the difficulties that arise when mentoring is targeted at a specific policy objective, such as reducing crime. As highlighted in the Introduction, it is asking a lot from interventions of this nature to turn people's lives around (Colley 2003). There is a risk that, because the headline policy objectives are not met, the relationships will be deemed to be a failure and that the gains made in other areas will be overlooked. Philip and Spratt (2007) argue that these studies show the potential of mentoring to assist young people to develop better relationships with their social networks and believe that 'this important but often overlooked aspect of mentoring could hold considerable promise for professional interventions in the social welfare field' (p.47). Rather than concluding that mentoring is not effective in the area of youth justice, it may be more apt to view it as an intervention that, if properly implemented, has the potential to support young people involved in or at risk of involvement in crime to improve aspects of their lives. However, mentoring is just one element of a range of supports that is required.

Case example 5.2: Adil (15 years)

Adil was 15 when he was referred to the mentoring programme by a social worker. Adil's life had been difficult. He fought a lot with his mum and eventually moved out from home and into voluntary care when he was 14. Part of the conflict with his mother was about his friends whom she didn't like. They got into trouble with the police for vandalism and anti-social behaviour and had received a number of warnings. Adil was not sure if he would enjoy the mentoring. He was matched with John, a 30-year-old mechanic. They were both interested in Manchester United and liked motorbikes so they used to talk a lot about those things. Adil didn't turn up for some of his meetings with John. He might be with his friends and forget all about it. The caseworker asked him to make more of an effort, which he did for a while because he liked John and he didn't want to let his caseworker down. He enjoyed meeting John but felt that he got more of a buzz from hanging around with his own friends. After about seven months, Adil decided he had had enough and asked to end the match. He enjoyed it while it lasted but he doesn't think it made a big difference to his life.

Key reading

Jolliffe, D. and Farrington, D.P. (2008) *The Influence of Mentoring on Reoffending.* Stockholm: National Council for Crime Prevention. Available at www.bra.se/extra/pod?action=pod_show&id=6&module_instance=11&offset=20, accessed on 18 July 2011.

Mentoring and Befriending Foundation (2011) *Research Summary 10: Reducing Offending.* Available at www.mandbf.org.uk/wp-content/uploads/2011/03/Research-summary-10-reducing-offending.pdf, accessed on 28 June 2011.

Philip, K. and Spratt, J. (2007) *A Synthesis of Published Research on Mentoring and Befriending.* Edinburgh: Mentoring and Befriending Foundation.

Young people leaving care
The function of social support for young people leaving the care system

Young people leaving care have specific vulnerabilities and stresses which require social support from family if available and other informal important sources in their lives. In particular their need for durable supporters who will 'stick with' them through their transition from care to independent living is obvious, but also the importance of having a strong source of concrete or practical support can sometimes be overlooked. For example, young people leaving care need support in acquiring independent living skills such as how to cook a wholesome meal, manage on a tight weekly budget and seek a place in further education or lodgings to rent. Having someone who is reliable and can reciprocate support informally including spontaneous acts of assistance and a capacity to share a joke can be seen as miniscule issues but in fact are known to be key (Clayden and Stein 2005). Apart from strong practical support, young people leaving care need robust emotional ties and connectivity with others. They need relationships like this not only with a range of family members and friends (including those with whom they lived while in care – foster carers, staff and/or fellow residents) with whom they have a sense of closeness, but also with at least one or two other people. Finally, the pursuance of leisure and hobby activities for care leavers which enables them create new sources of social support can be a strong antidote to the typical risk of feeling lonely and isolated on leaving care (Gilligan 2009).

How can a mentor best support a young care leaver?

Mentor supporters for care leavers can offer regular educational, emotional, social and practical help. Apart from being there as a reliable friend for the young person, a mentor can offer supportive and constructive advice if and when needed. Young people who have been through the care system and successfully go on to third-level education and or employment often find themselves as having capacity to mentor a young person in care sometimes in the same placement (residential centre or foster care) as they attended. This has the added value of their being 'veteran supporters' who have lived the experiences that the mentee is experiencing and puts them in the unique position as mentors of having real grounded knowledge of the stresses the care leaver is facing (Stein 2005). Sometimes this can have an added bonus of allowing adult mentor care leavers to retain positive contact with those they knew while in care themselves. There is also growing interest in the development of peer mentoring and befriending for both young people in care and care leavers, whereby positive mutually supportive relationships are created to enable young people to support each other through the in-care and leaving care process.

What are the key elements of a successful mentoring programme to support care leavers?

Key elements to the success of in-care or leaving care programmes relate to good sustainable relationships and not just at the mentor and mentee levels. First, mentors need to be carefully matched with mentees. If the mentor and mentee do not share common interests (which can be identified in the assessment process) the relationship will simply 'dry up' or worse, leave the mentee feeling more isolated (Clayden and Stein 2005). Regular 'checking in' by the case manager on the status and progress of the relationship is key for both the mentor and mentee. The mentor is not a professional but acting as a friend and there is a strong risk relating to mentoring for care leavers that the donor of support can become over-involved or over-burdened by the problems and stresses that the mentee is enduring. Additionally, the supportive relationship between the primary care-giver (parent, workers or foster carer) and the mentor is vital. Where this relationship is based on parity of esteem with a sense of 'informal comradeship' or being in this together for the young person, successful outcomes are more likely to accrue. Conversely if the residential social carer or foster carer sees the mentor as a threat to his or her role or undermining his or her relationship with the young person, this can have very negative effects for all concerned.

Finally the issue of safe care practices and risks of abuse and or allegations of abuse both in mentoring and in residential and foster care have come to the fore strongly in recent decades, particularly in northern Europe and the USA. So guarantees of safety are essential – not just for the young person in or leaving care, but also for mentors and particularly those who choose to befriend youth who are vulnerable.

Case example 5.3: David (17 years)

David left care at 17 years of age having been in long-term foster care in a rural town. He moved to a city to commence university and, although he retained contact with both his family and foster carers, he quickly developed a sense of isolation in part emerging from his finding it difficult to mix with other students. In particular David felt awkward about having been in care and others asking him questions about it. Michael, his mentor and a final year student in the university, spent three hours per week (on average) with David. Michael offered David a lot of practical advice on getting more involved in the university as well as some help with learning techniques even though they were studying very different subjects. In addition, Michael and David shared an interest in drama and together joined the university drama society's production of the Neil Simon play *The Odd Couple*, both taking minor parts in the production and helping with the set design two evenings a week. This in itself enabled their development of mutual interests and support from Michael enabled David to develop new, fellow 'thespian' friends. In addition, David used his mentor Michael to discuss keeping up contact with his family and foster carers; contact tended to wax and wane for David. The mentoring relationship lasted formally until Michael graduated, but three years later both David and Michael are still in regular e-mail and phone contact and meet occasionally.

Key reading

Clayden, J. and Stein, M. (2005) *Mentoring Young People Leaving Care: Someone for Me.* York: Joseph Rowntree Foundation.

Gilligan, R. (2009) *Promoting Resilience: Supporting Children and Young People who are in Care, Adopted or in Need* (2nd edition). London: British Association for Adoption and Fostering.

Stein, M. (2005) *Resilience and Young People Leaving Care: Overcoming the Odds.* York: Joseph Rowntree Foundation.

Asylum-seekers, refugees and migrants

The Children's Society in the UK undertook research with young refugees in the London borough of Newham to understand their perspectives regarding the range of factors that help them to feel settled in their new community. The Children's Society describes settlement as 'the process of trying to establish in a new country through the acquisition of basic needs such as language, education, security and stable accommodation. It involves the building of networks and planning for the future' (2006, p.9). Young participants in the study identified factors such as learning the language, securing their legal status, attending school, becoming involved in local networks, feeling safe and secure and being part of a religious community as the things that helped them to feel settled. Young people also identified the need for compassionate people or organisations that they could turn to for advice, support, information and understanding. Young people referred to the importance of foster parents, carers, friends and teachers as offering invaluable support to their sustainable settlement and development and giving them a sense of security. Being able to build up trust with somebody was considered to be a key factor in the pursuit of settlement.

This research highlights the considerable potential for mentoring interventions to support refugee, asylum-seeker and immigrant young people in settling into new communities. Mentoring has the potential to support young people in the following ways:

- *Practical support:* explaining the cultures, traditions and systems of the country, helping with bureaucracy, acting as a mediator where appropriate, introducing the young person to local cultural attractions and recreational opportunities, providing support with learning the language if required.

- *Emotional support:* providing a listening ear, showing empathy and understanding, building up trust.

- *Advice support:* advising on ways to deal with particular issues.

- *Esteem support:* providing positive feedback to the young person on their achievements and abilities.

Research has shown that refugees and asylum-seekers are likely to experience poorer mental health than native populations. Mentoring and befriending has been recommended as a means of combating isolation and preventing the onset of mental health problems (Petevi 1996).

All of the mentoring models – adult, school-based and peer – described in this book can be meaningfully employed to support young people with their settlement in a new environment. There is considerable scope for peer mentoring, whereby young people are matched with a same age or older peer. These peers can help young people to connect with their social network and understand the school system and can generally support them with settling into their new community. Based on the research referred to above, The Children's Society (2006) recommended that schools and voluntary organisations facilitate peer mentoring as a support for young refugees. The one-to-one classic model of mentoring is also likely to be of benefit to young people as there are specific types of support which are best provided by an adult (for example, adults may have a better grasp of the local bureaucracy than a peer). Because settling into a new school and dealing with the complexities of the education system are such onerous tasks, there is a value in school-based mentoring, whether undertaken by mentors or peers. Research by the Refugee Council (2008) recommended the establishment of mentoring and befriending services for refugee and asylum-seekers, particularly for separated children, to help with their educational needs.

Mentoring for refugees, asylum-seekers and immigrants can be provided through general community or school-based mentoring programmes or through specific targeted programmes. Non-targeted community-based programmes have the potential to reach young refugees, asylum-seekers or immigrants who may feel isolated in their communities and, as well as offering the one-to-one support of a mentor, can introduce mentees to the other mentored youth and adults, thus extending their social network. Targeted programmes are valuable in areas where there are sufficient numbers of young people to merit having stand-alone programmes.

Case example 5.4: Chinara (14 years)

Chinara came to the UK from Nigeria in 2007 as a result of unrest in her home country, which made it difficult for her to stay. She had never been out of her home country before and felt very lonely and afraid on her arrival. Chinara was living in a hostel with other young people who did not have family in the UK. She was assigned a social worker who was very helpful in helping her to find a school and introduced her to a youth worker. The youth worker invited Chinara to some groups where she got to meet some local people. Through this group, she heard about a mentoring programme and decided to apply as she thought it would be nice to have an adult to talk to on a regular basis. She got on well with her social worker but the social worker was very busy and was not usually available at the weekends. Through the mentoring programme, Chinara was matched with Fiona. Fiona was 26 and was working in a bank. They had a lot in common and their friendship developed quickly. They enjoyed going window shopping, looking at magazines and going to the cinema. Chinara had a lot of questions about life in England which Fiona could answer. Chinara was doing well at school but was unsure of how to go about applying for college. Fiona explained how the system worked and helped her with her application. Fiona was very interested in learning about Chinara's culture and Chinara enjoyed telling her stories from home. Chinara still felt lonely and missed her family and friends but she was glad to have Fiona's support, which helped her to feel more settled in her new environment.

Key reading

Children's Society, The (2006) *Making a New Life in Newham*. London: The Children's Society.

Mentoring and Befriending Foundation (2011a) *Research Summary 2: Asylum Seekers, Refugees and Migrants*. Available at www.mandbf.org.uk/wp-content/uploads/2011/03/Research-summary-2-asylum-seekers-refugees-and-migrants.pdf, accessed on 28 June 2011.

Mentoring youth with a disability

One of the key issues facing young people with a disability is overcoming societal barriers that can prevent their full participation in family, school, community and civic society. Mentoring programmes involving young people with disabilities can help to support greater social participation and enhance the young person's independence from family and carers. Research has shown that successful mentoring programmes can improve independent living skills among mentees (Bethel 2003). To achieve this, it is important that the mentor adopts an enabling role, focusing on the needs and wishes of the mentee. There is a risk that mentors may have a disabling influence whereby they are directive regarding what the young person needs, and feel that it is their role to do things for the young person rather than enable them to do things for themselves. A key function of the mentoring relationship, therefore, is that of normalisation so as to ensure non-stigmatisation and enhance and promote ability rather than any disability for the mentee.

Young people with disabilities can be involved in the full spectrum of mentoring programmes, including the classic adult–youth model, peer mentoring and group mentoring. Where appropriate, targeted mentoring programmes for youth with a disability may focus on activities such as sports, drama or music, while other programmes can have particular objectives, for example to counteract the risk of bullying in schools. While there may be differences in the task and context of the mentoring relationship depending on the nature of the programme, the need for mutual friendship based on parity of esteem, warmth and trust remains critical. When we return to our principle of TEA as a model for types of support (see Chapter 1), the need for consistent positive emotional support as well as for tangible help, advice and esteem support are seen to be relevant. Like in all mentoring relationships, mutual engagement in enjoyable activities is very important in terms of building the relationship. Mentoring programmes which enable supportive friendships and social stability can also lead to enhanced personal skills for the mentee, such as better motivation and stronger self-confidence, as well as being better able to express feelings and demonstrate interpersonal skills. Furthermore, mentoring relationships characterised by reciprocity ensure that young people have the opportunity to give support to others as well as being supported themselves, thus showing the young person that he or she can play an important role in society. This is noteworthy as the role of youth with a disability as civic contributors can often be overlooked. The issues of adequate and proper rights and services for youth with a disability are present in most societies and, through a mentoring relationship, youth mentees can be supported to advocate for what is duly theirs if they wish to do so.

Case example 5.5: Mary (16 years)

Since Mary (16 years, with a mild intellectual disability) commenced weekly contact with her mentor Jane, just over a year ago, she states that her world has been transformed. Apart from taking her to the cinema every month, usually to see the latest 'movie release', Jane has introduced Mary to traditional Irish music and more particularly has taught her how to play a number of traditional tunes on the tin whistle – which Mary really likes. More recently Mary has started to attend a music session in a local pub from 6 to 8 pm every second Thursday and joins in with other session musicians there. Though they play a little fast for her at times, Mary manages fine by sticking with the first half of the tune and opting out of the second if, as she states, 'the going gets tough'. Furthermore, every Monday of the week of the session Mary and Jane meet up to practise Mary's set of tunes for the forthcoming session. Apart from making a new set of friends at the sessions, Mary has started to teach two of her friends, both with a similar disability, how to play 'St Anne's Reel' and 'The Girl who Broke my Heart' on the tin whistle. Jane states that she really enjoys being a mentor to Mary and that she gets back more than she gives, not least of which from Mary's energy and positiveness which Jane describes as 'a constant source of joy to her'. Apart from the enjoyable activities they do together Mary calls Jane 'a real pal'. Jane and Mary are planning to perform together at the mentor and mentees' party at Halloween.

Key reading

Bethel, J. (2003) 'Our Life, Our Say': An Evaluation of a Young Disabled People's Peer Mentoring/ Support Project. York: Joseph Rowntree Foundation.

Intergenerational mentoring

Over the past decade in particular, intergenerational programmes have become increasingly popular. These programmes have been developed as a result of an awareness of how interaction between older and younger generations can be mutually beneficial for both parties. Historically, the nature of society meant that intergenerational interaction happened informally on a daily basis, with skills and knowledge being passed from the older to the younger generation and vice versa. In today's society, however, many older and younger people don't have opportunities to interact. Intergenerational mentoring programmes have been designed to provide opportunities for older and younger people to learn from and support each other. Both older people and younger people often have time on their hands, have a range of valuable skills and may experience isolation or loneliness. Intergenerational mentoring can match them with each other to benefit from mutual support. A key feature of intergenerational mentoring is that it is two-way – it is assumed that the older person will equally learn from the younger person. Hatton-Yeo and Telfer (2008, p.4) define intergenerational practice as 'bringing people from different generations together in purposeful, mutually beneficial activities which promote greater understanding and respect and contribute to building more cohesive communities.'

Adults aged 50 or older are generally considered to be the 'older' generation, while the younger generation can include children, young people and young adults. Intergenerational mentoring programmes can focus on specific skills such as reading and literacy or they can be based around support and friendship. The support can be practical in terms of learning particular skills. For example, older people can demonstrate crafts, cooking and reading, while younger people can impart computer, phone and internet skills. Emotional and esteem support can also be shared through telling stories, listening to experiences and offering reassurance. The self-esteem of both parties can be enhanced by feeling that they have something valuable to contribute to society.

Granville and Laidlaw (2000) reported on an intergenerational programme which matched young offenders with older people in care settings. As part of their community service, the young people visited elderly people in their care homes. The research showed that the older people enjoyed the company of the young people as they brought fresh perspectives into their lives. Granville and Laidlaw see a role for such programmes in reducing negative stereotyping and discrimination and promoting social cohesiveness.

Research has shown that participation in intergenerational programmes is generally perceived as enjoyable and has led to the development of friendships and greater understanding between participants. Older people gained improved health and well-being, reduced isolation and a greater sense of self-worth, while young people were found to have gained in specific skills and increased their self-esteem (Springate et al. 2008).

The guidelines for good practice described in Chapter 3 are also relevant in the case of intergenerational mentoring programmes. There is a need for rigorous assessment, careful matching and ongoing supervision to ensure that the match is progressing well. As with all relationships, it is more likely to be successful if a genuine bond develops between the adult and young person. The benefits that accrue will also depend on the duration and intensity of the relationship. If the programme is short-lived it is probably unlikely that there will be long-term benefits.

Case example 5.6: Martha

Martha took early retirement from her job as a teacher and was anxious to keep engaged and active. She missed the energy and optimism of the young people she used to teach, so when she saw an advertisement for an intergenerational reading programme, she knew it was for her. She was matched with Kisha, a 10-year-old girl from a local school. They met twice a week at school where Martha helped Kisha with her reading. When they were finished, they chatted about what was going on in both of their lives. Martha saw an improvement in Kisha's reading and enjoyed hearing about her life. She does not feel that they became very close and senses that Kisha was a little inhibited in talking to her, possibly because of the age gap between them and because she was a former teacher.

Key reading

Hatton-Yeo, A. and Telfer, S. (2008) *A Guide to Mentoring Across Generations.* Glasgow: The Scottish Centre for Intergenerational Practice.

Mentoring and Befriending Foundation (2010) *Research Summary 8: Intergenerational Activity.* Manchester. Available at www.mandbf.org.uk/wp-content/uploads/2011/03/Research-summary-8-intergenerational.pdf.

Conclusion

In this chapter, issues relating to how best to support six specific groups of young people have been explored, with core messages for mentors and mentoring services highlighted throughout. As indicated at the outset, it is not possible to cover all adversities which youth and their families face, but it is likely that the messages contained in the case examples will be applicable in other contexts.

References

Bethel, J. (2003) *'Our Life, Our Say': An Evaluation of a Young Disabled People's Peer Mentoring/ Support Project*. York: Joseph Rowntree Foundation.

Brugha, T.S. (1995) 'Social Support and Psychiatric Disorder: Recommendations for Clinical Practice and Research.' In T.S. Brugha (ed.) *Social Support and Psychiatric Disorder, Research Findings and Guidelines for Clinical Practice*. Cambridge: Cambridge University Press.

Children's Society, The (2006) *Making a New Life in Newham*. London: The Children's Society.

Clayden, J. and Stein, M. (2005) *Mentoring Young People Leaving Care: Someone for Me*. York: Joseph Rowntree Foundation.

Colley, H. (2003) *Mentoring for Social Inclusion*. London: Routledge Falmer.

Gilligan, R. (2009) *Promoting Resilience: Supporting Children and Young People who are in Care, Adopted or in Need* (2nd edition). London: British Association for Adoption and Fostering.

Granville, G. and Laidlaw, J. (2000) *A Partnership of Trust: Young Offenders Supporting Older People in Care Settings: An Example of Social Inclusion through Inter-generational Practice*. London: Beth Johnson Foundation.

Hatton-Yeo, A. and Telfer, S. (2008) *A Guide to Mentoring Across Generations*. Glasgow: The Scottish Centre for Intergenerational Practice.

Jolliffe, D. and Farrington, D.P. (2008) *The Influence of Mentoring on Reoffending*. Stockholm: National Council for Crime Prevention. Available at www.bra.se/extra/pod?action=pod_show&id=6&module_instance=11&offset=20, accessed on 18 July 2011.

Mead, N., Lester, H. and Chew-Graham, L.G. (2010) 'Effects of befriending on depressive symptoms and distress: Systematic review and meta-analysis.' *The British Journal of Psychiatry 196*, 96–101.

Mentoring and Befriending Foundation (2011a) *Research Summary 2: Asylum Seekers, Refugees and Migrants*. Available at www.mandbf.org/wp-content/uploads/2011/03/Research-summary-2-asylum-seekers-refugees-and-migrants.pdf, accessed on 28 June 2011.

Mentoring and Befriending Foundation (2011b) *Research Summary 10: Reducing Offending*. Available at www.mandbf.org/wp-content/uploads/2011/03/Research-summary-10-reducing-offending.pdf, accessed on 28 June 2011.

Newburn, T. and Shiner, M. (2005) *Dealing with Disaffection: Young People, Mentoring, and Social Inclusion*. Cullompton: Willan Publishing.

Petevi, M. (1996) 'Forced Displacement: Refugee Trauma, Protection and Assistance.' In Y. Danieli, N. Rodney and L. Weisaeth (eds) *International Responses to Traumatic Stress*. United Nations Publication. New York: Baywood Publishing Company.

Philip, K. and Spratt, J. (2007) *A Synthesis of Published Research on Mentoring and Befriending*. Edinbugh: Mentoring and Befriending Foundation.

Refugee Council (2008) *Beyond the School Gates: Supporting Refugees and Asylum Seekers in Secondary School*. London: Refugee Council. Available at: www.refugeecouncil.org. uk/Resources/Refugee%20Council/downloads/researchreports/inclusiveschools_ may08.pdf, accessed on 28 June 2011.

Sipe, C.L. (2002) 'Mentoring programs for adolescents: A research summary.' *Journal of Adolescent Health 31*, 251–260.

Springate, I., Atkinson, M. and Martin, K. (2008) *Intergenerational Practice: A Review of the Literature*. Local Government Association Research Report F/SR262. Slough: National Foundation for Educational Research.

St James-Roberts, I., Greenlaw, G., Simon, A. and Hurry, J. (2005) *National Evaluation of Youth Justice Board Mentor Programmes for Young People who have Offended or are at Risk of Offending*. London: Youth Justice Board.

Stein, M. (2005) *Resilience and Young People Leaving Care: Overcoming the Odds*. York: Joseph Rowntree Foundation.

Conclusion

Introduction

Mentoring programmes aim to create a supportive friendship between a young person and an adult in which trust and closeness can develop and the adult can help the young person to cope and develop to the best of his or her abilities. The central thesis of this book is that mentoring can be a valuable source of support to young people, particularly those facing adversity or difficulty in their lives. This book has endeavoured to provide a simple overview of the theory, research and practice of youth mentoring and to summarise key aspects of social support theory in order to illustrate the ways in which mentoring relationships can support young people. In particular, we have emphasised the types of support that young people benefit from, the qualities and features of such support and highlight how mentoring programmes can create the conditions for beneficial relationships to develop. We have also explored some of the contexts within which mentoring can occur.

As we saw in the Introduction, there is a strong rationale for the existence of mentoring programmes in modern societies. It has been argued that young people don't have as much opportunity to form relationships with adults in their communities as they did in previous generations because of changes in the nature of family and community lives over recent decades. Yet studies of young people who have thrived in spite of significant adversity highlight how access to the support of a non-parental adult can be an important asset in the lives of resilient youth. As well as having a theoretical rationale, there are practical benefits to services of this nature. While they are provided in the context of a professional service, they represent a flexible, informal form of intervention that can provide support to young people outside office hours and in the contexts of their lives. Furthermore, research has shown that young people are more likely to develop trust in and open up to informal supporters than professionals.

The messages from research relating to young people and social support are unambiguous. In simple terms, the more support that young people have, the better they can cope. Conversely, those with less access to supportive relationships can find it more difficult to cope. While the importance of support is clear, providing effective support for young people can be complex. Chapter 1 aimed to unpack the concept of social support as it relates to young people, highlighting the importance of the various types of support for particular purposes (tangible, emotional, esteem and advice) and the particular qualities of support that hold the key to whether it is likely to be effective in achieving its desired outcome. For example, we saw the importance of closeness, durability and reciprocity in supportive relationships and the risks associated with ties that are critical.

In Chapter 2, some practical ways in which the support available to young people can be assessed were introduced. The toolkit outlined is designed to address one of the criticisms of mentoring – the tendency to assume that a mentor is needed for all vulnerable young people regardless of their existing support network. These tools can help practitioners in deciding whether mentoring is appropriate for a particular young person in the first place or whether they have sufficient but untapped support in their natural network. The tools may also be used alongside mentoring interventions to facilitate the young person to enlist additional support from his or her network. They can also be used when a mentoring relationship is coming to an end to put in place a support plan for young people, thus ensuring that they are not left 'high and dry' when their mentoring relationship ends.

Thanks to the significant increase in mentoring research over the past decade in particular, there is now a solid body of evidence regarding the practices that are associated with better outcomes from mentoring programmes. First and foremost, the protection of children and young people is critical and so it is imperative that mentoring programmes are run in a safe way, highlighting the importance of mentor recruitment practices and ongoing supervision. In a time of worldwide resource constraints, it is also important that programmes are effective. There are clear guidelines regarding the practices associated with effectiveness in mentoring. These include rigorous assessment of mentors and young people, careful matching, training and ongoing support for mentors and attentive supervision. Again, reflecting the fact that the most supportive relationships are close, durable and characterised by reciprocity, mentoring programmes must endeavour to ensure that matches are facilitated to last as long as possible and become as close as possible, and that mentors adopt a developmental approach rather than a prescriptive approach. It is advisable for mentoring programmes to monitor key indicators associated with quality and to put in place ongoing measures of key outcomes they would like to achieve. Those wishing to start a new mentoring programme can draw upon the excellent resources developed for this purpose by MENTOR in the USA, the Mentoring and Befriending Foundation in the UK and the Australian and New Zealand youth mentoring organisations referred to in the Useful Contacts section at the end of the book.

While the majority of the book refers to the classic one-to-one model of community-based mentoring, we see in Chapters 4 and 5 that mentoring can be usefully applied in a range of contexts and with young people with specific needs. The practice of mentoring in schools has become increasingly popular. School-based mentoring can take the form of cross-age peer mentoring, whereby older students mentor younger students as they start secondary school. This form of mentoring is seen to bring benefits to both mentors and mentees. For many mentors, it is their first experience of volunteering or formally helping another and the experience can help to develop their sense of identity as civic actors. Young people have benefited from such programmes in terms of greater connectedness to school, which may make them more likely to settle and do well academically. School mentoring can also be undertaken by adults. Research into this form of mentoring shows that it can bring academic benefits and greater school connectedness in the short term but there is no evidence that these benefits are sustained beyond involvement in the programme. Like community-based programmes, school-based programmes must be adequately structured and ensure that the mentees receive enough mentoring to make a real difference to them.

Mentoring has been targeted at particular policy obje such as reducing offending behaviour among young people aiding with the social inclusion of young people with a disabil In Chapter 5, six examples are given of specific contexts in which mentoring can take place and some of the nuances associated with mentoring for particular groups of young people are highlighted. For example, we see that mentoring has great potential in the settlement of refugee and asylum-seeking young people and can work in various ways to support young people with mental health problems. Again, the nuances associated with the effective provision of support are of relevance. For example, young people leaving care need supporters who will be there for them on an ongoing basis (durable) and who can empathise with the journey they have travelled.

Closing policy considerations

This book has explored the connection between social support enlistment and youth mentoring from an evidence and practice intervention perspective. However, social research and service provision do not occur in isolation to wider policy and it would be remiss of the authors not to give some consideration to this issue. So finally, although this book is not intended as a policy reader, closing remarks follow that consider very briefly some of the future research evidence, policy and practice implementation agenda.

1. The importance of informal social support

The central function of informal sources of help in the lives of children and youth experiencing adversity has been well recognised, not just by social support theorists such as Cutrona (2000) but elsewhere including academics from youth, social work and community development sectors. In the 1980s informal social support was neatly described by Garbarino (1983) as the 'bread and butter of relationships' (p.v). Apart from any research evidence on the benefits of informal support, its importance is obvious, simply because we all survive on the strength of exchanged natural support from others including family and friendships. In general, it is only when this natural pool of help is unavailable or unwilling to assist that we turn to professional services for help. Although mentoring occurs in the context of a professional programme, it is important to value the 'pure informal friendship' factor in mentoring and not to see mentors as 'quasi-professionals in sheep's clothing'. So whereas mentoring programmes may seek desired outcomes such as reduced anti-social behaviour or less drug taking by youth, mentors should be valued as good friends who help young people in need, rather than therapists.

2. The role of evidence in youth mentoring

The level of evidence for mentoring has received much attention within the research literature (Rhodes and DuBois 2006). Since the well cited Public-Private Ventures research in the mid-1990s in respect of the Big Brothers Big Sisters programme in the USA (Tierney *et al.* 1995), in particular, much attention has been paid to the use of experimental design methodologies. For example, experimental design research in Ireland on the Foróige Big Brothers Big Sisters has followed this trend (Dolan *et al.* 2011). While the findings of these studies have contributed enormously to our understanding of the impact of mentoring and the practices associated with more effective programmes, it is important that mentoring research is not dominated by this form of research design on the basis that the question of randomised control trials being a best 'fit for purpose' methodology for youth mentoring has not been fully debated (O'Regan 2010; Philip *et al.* 2004). An obvious risk is that the unforgiving nature of this research design may mean that the organic and fluid nature of the factors that make mentoring fail or succeed may not be understood.

In contrast to the impact-focused studies, qualitative mentoring research studies, particularly those from the UK, aim to understand the 'journey travelled' (Stein 2007) and have been valuable in illustrating the movement between the instrumental and the expressive in mentoring relationships (Philip 1997; Philip and Hendry 1996). Furthermore, Philip (2007) argues that the outcomes prioritised from mentoring schemes for children living in disadvantage or in troubled circumstances are often measured in terms of 'moving up and moving out' indicators, which can lead us to overlook the 'horizontal' gains that might be achieved through mentoring. In qualitative studies, young people frequently refer to better relationships with parents or siblings as the main benefits from mentoring, but these may not be picked up where 'top-down' indicators of success are identified. Philip and Hendry (2000) argue that there is an assumption that there is a commonly agreed standard to be reached and that the question of standards is unproblematic.

We must never lose sight of the fact that the core function of youth mentoring is the pursuit of natural relationship development and maintenance. The future challenge for mentoring research is to develop research designs that can capture the human connectivity of mentoring relationships, while simultaneously contributing the evidence required for policy making. Mixed-methods studies may offer a means through which this can be achieved but further work is required to identify how best qualitative and quantitative approaches can best be sequenced and integrated (Brady and O'Regan 2009).

3. Youth mentoring and the armour of prevention and early intervention

School- and community-based youth mentoring, like parenting programmes, form part of the range of prevention and early (in the problem) interventions gaining increasing international recognition. However, very often it is the much more expensive services such as secure residential care or high support units for youth that receive funding. It is somewhat ironic that even though the outcomes for youth who attend such services are generally very poor, and care placements are incredibly expensive, youth mentoring, which is relatively much cheaper and now has evidence of modest outcomes, struggles for funding investment. Just like the argument for early years services, youth mentoring has cost and social benefit potential but needs time and investment to be allowed grow. Positive change requires politicians with responsibility for children and youth, service designers and policy-makers to show leadership and a leap of faith. They must not just react in emergency response mode to the latest crisis by seeking to abate rather than solve long-term problems. Just as Mark Twain said, everybody talks about the weather but no one does anything about it – a similar view should not be taken to strong investment in prevention (which everyone also agrees with).

4. A rights-based and youth-led agenda

From a rights-based perspective, if youth mentoring is proven to be one of a series of effective interventions in working with young people and families who experience adversities, it could be argued that young people are entitled to it as a service. From the point of view of implementation of Article 12 of the UNCRC (as indicated in Chapter 2), the right for young people to participate in mentoring programmes should be upheld as an option. Were the mentoring relationship to fail, as will sometimes be the case because mentoring is not a panacea, at least it has been tried ahead of any more serious and costly intervention. Importantly, the young person's civic and human right to participation and to an early intervention service would have been upheld.

5. Youth mentoring standing alone or part of other interventions?

Finally, in the context of looking to the future and what will work best for young people in need, the question of whether youth mentoring should be a stand-alone intervention or an integral part of youth work services, deserves some brief consideration. Certainly the Irish study on Foróige's BBBS found value in the latter, in that young people benefited from mentoring as an add-on to youth work. This research found that youth derived support both from attending their weekly youth work project and from regular contact with their mentor.

Many countries which face the global economic crisis require innovation in every sector of society and this is the case within the context of youth services provision. Youth who have value to civic society today in their own right will similarly have importance into the future as adults. Common sense would suggest that ensuring youth mentoring is provided in the most cost effective (recession proof) way is important. More importantly for young people it is crucial that youth mentoring is 'part of' and not 'apart from' every aspect of their lives within family, school, community, service and societal contexts.

References

Brady, B and O'Regan, C. (2009) 'Meeting the challenge of doing an RCT evaluation of youth mentoring in Ireland: A journey in mixed methods.' *Journal of Mixed Methods Research 3*, 3, 265–280.

Cutrona, C.E. (2000) 'Social Support Principles for Strengthening Families: Messages from America.' In J. Canavan, P. Dolan and J. Pinkerton (eds) *Family Support Direction from Diversity.* London: Jessica Kingsley Publishers.

Dolan, P., Brady, B., O'Regan, C., Russell, D., Canavan, J. and Forkan, C. (2011) *Big Brothers Big Sisters of Ireland: Evaluation Study. Report One: Randomised Controlled Trial and Implementation Report.* Galway: Child and Family Research Centre.

Garbarino, J. (1983) 'Social Support Networks: RX for the Helping Professionals.' In J.K. Whittaker and J. Garbarino (eds) *Social Support Networks: Informal Helping in the Human Services.* New York: Aldine de Gruyter.

O'Regan C. (2010) 'Methodology and evidence in evaluation: Lessons from a randomised control trial of a youth mentoring programme in Ireland.' UNESCO Child and Family Research Centre, School of Political Science and Sociology, NUI Galway, Ireland (unpublished doctoral thesis).

Philip, K. (1997) 'New perspectives on mentoring: Young people, youth work and mentoring.' University of Aberdeen (unpublished PhD dissertation).

Philip, K. (2007) Paper presented at the ESRC Seminar Series, *Researching Youth Mentoring – Building Theory and Building Evidence.* Aberdeen: The Rowan Group.

Philip, K. and Hendry, L.B. (1996) 'Young people and mentoring: Towards a typology.' *Journal of Adolescence 19*, 189–201.

Philip, K. and Hendry, L.B. (2000) 'Making sense of mentoring or mentoring making sense? Reflections on the mentoring process by adult mentors with young people.' *Journal of Community & Applied Social Psychology 10*, 3, 211–223.

Philip, K., Shucksmith, J. and King, C. (2004) *Sharing a Laugh? A Qualitative Study of Mentoring Interventions with Young People.* York: Joseph Rowntree Foundation.

Rhodes, J.E. and DuBois, D.L. (2006) 'Understanding and facilitating the youth mentoring movement.' *Social Policy Report 20*, 3, 3–19.

Stein, M. (2007) Paper presented at the ESRC Seminar Series, *Researching Youth Mentoring – Building Theory and Building Evidence.* Aberdeen: The Rowan Group.

Tierney, J., Grossman, J. and Resch, N. (1995) *Making a Difference: An Impact Study of Big Brothers Big Sisters of America.* Philadelphia, PA: Public-Private Ventures.

Useful Contacts

Australian Youth Mentoring Network
www.youthmentoring.org.au

Big Brothers Big Sisters of America
www.bbbs.org

Foróige/Big Brothers Big Sisters of Ireland
www.bbbsireland.ie

Mentoring and Befriending Foundation (UK)
www.mandbf.org.uk

MENTOR/National Mentoring Partnership (USA)
www.mentoring.org

Scottish Mentoring Network
www.scottishmentoringnetwork.co.uk

New Zealand Youth Mentoring Network
www.youthmentoring.org.nz

Subject Index

Author Index